"When God comes to rule in the heart of a person, the ethics of Jesus are worked out in his daily life."

"Jesus changed the tense of the rule of God to the present."

"Love never looks more like a winner than when it is defeated."

"The character of God is such that he cannot work in the life of the self-righteous."

"Whatever a person thinks about God largely determines that person's ministry and mission."

Who Rules Your Life?

Exploring the Kingdom Parables of Jesus

Prentice A. Meador, Jr.

JOURNEY BOOKS

An SPC Publication
Austin, Texas 78765

A complete Teacher's Manual/Resource Kit for use with this paperback is available from your religious bookstore or the publisher.

WHO RULES YOUR LIFE?
Copyright © 1979 by Sweet Publishing Company,
Austin, Texas 78765.

Unless otherwise indicated, scripture quotations are from The HOLY BIBLE New International Version, New Testament, Copyright © 1978 by New York International Bible Society, and used by permission.

Edited by Harold Straughn and Roger Hornbaker
Cover designed by Tom Williams

Printed in the U.S.A.
Library of Congress Catalog Card Number 79-64089
ISBN 0-8344-0107-X
5 4 3 2 1

Contents

Preface

Jesus begins his Galilean ministry by talking about the "good news of God." He announces, "The time has come. The kingdom of God is near. Repent and believe the good news!" (Mark 1:14, 15). This announcement establishes a basic touchstone of his ministry—the kingdom of God.

But what is the kingdom of God? Of course, there are many features of the kingdom, features previewed in Old Testament prophecy that are developed more fully in the New Testament. Historically, the words rule, kingdom, or dominion include both the art of ruling over and that which is ruled. In a general sense, the kingdom of God encompasses all of the work and preaching of Jesus Christ, his apostles, and his people. More definitely, the kingdom is present in Jesus. He is the rule of God, the good news, the new thing God has done. When a person accepts Jesus Christ in his life, the kingdom, or the rule of God, reigns in the heart of that person. This is the point Jesus makes when he says, "The kingdom of God does not come visibly, nor will people say 'Here it is,' or 'There it is,' because the kingdom of God is within you" (Luke 17:20, 21).

The *rule* of God is, then, the creative, dynamic activity of God in the life of a person when he obeys Jesus as Savior and Lord. Jesus uses parables to give us a better understanding of how this happens.

Introduction

A Definition

Since I was a child, I have heard a parable defined as "an earthly story with a heavenly meaning." I don't know who came up with that definition, but it's not a bad one. For heaven and earth do meet in the parables of Jesus.

A parable is a particular type of metaphor or simile. Like all figures of speech, it "implies an intuitive perception of the similarity in dissimilars."[1] It is, as one writer says, "drawn from nature or common life"; and its power lies in its ability to "arrest the hearer by its vividness or strangeness, leaving the mind in sufficient doubt about its precise application to tease it into active thought."[2] A parable then, is a point of comparison between an accepted truth in the reality of the natural world and a new, similar truth in the reality of the spiritual world. Jesus made connections between events that are obvious in the natural world and the equally basic truths of the spiritual realm— how daily life intersects eternal truth. As Jesus offered the rule of God to people, he lifted them

11

from the routine, hum-drum, and dull thud of daily existence to a higher plane of abundant living. He used his parables as vehicles to accomplish his goal.

This book had its beginning in the summer of 1975 at Vanderbilt University Divinity Library, where I was preparing a special series of fall sermons on the parables of Jesus. I chose the parables because of their central importance in the teachings of Jesus. The parables make up more than one-third of Jesus' recorded teaching.[3] They are also perennially popular. The stories of the Good Samaritan and The Prodigal Son are among the best-loved stories of both children and adults. Jesus carefully wove his parables out of life and his teachings. And in his hands, the parable became a powerful instrument—compelling our closest attention.

List of Parables

The particular selection of parables included in this volume is based upon several measures. First, most scholars recognize these parables as full and complete, not mere figures of speech or epigrams of Jesus. Second, all these parables focus upon the kingdom, its proclamation and explanation. By this distinctive figure, the parable, Jesus conferred power and prominence upon the kingdom. Third, all parables under consideration here have their sources in Matthew, Mark, and Luke. Not included in this volume are the figurative sayings of Jesus such as "I am . . . . " statements recorded in the gospel of John. In this volume, the parables to be treated are the following:

Parable	Text
The Wise and Foolish Builders	Matthew 7:24-29
New Garment, New Wine Skin	Matthew 9:16-17; Mark 2:21-22; Luke 5:36-38
Sower	Matthew 13:3-8; Mark 4:3-8; Luke 8:5-8
Weeds	Matthew 13:24-30; 36-43
Mustard Seed and Yeast	Matthew 13:31-35; Mark 4:30-34; Luke 13:18-21
Hidden Treasure and Pearl	Matthew 13:44-46
Net	Matthew 13:47-52
Lost Sheep	Matthew 18:10-14; Luke 15:1-7
Unmerciful Servant	Matthew 18:21-35
Workers in the Vineyard	Matthew 20:1-16
Two Sons	Matthew 21:28-32
Tenants	Matthew 21:33-46; Mark 12:1-12; Luke 20:9-19
Wedding Banquet	Matthew 22:1-14
The Budding Fig Tree	Matthew 24:32-35; Mark 13:28-32
The Ten Virgins	Matthew 25:1-13
Talents	Matthew 25:14-30
Growing Seed	Mark 4:26-29
Two Debtors	Luke 7:36-50
Good Samaritan	Luke 10:25-37
The Persistent Host	Luke 11:5-10
The Unclean Spirit	Luke 11:24-26
Rich Fool	Luke 12:16-21
Steward with Supervision	Luke 12:42-46
The Barren Fig Tree	Luke 13:6-9
Great Banquet	Luke 14:15-24
The Tower Builder and King at War	Luke 14:28-32
Lost Coin	Luke 15:8-10
Lost Son	Luke 15:11-32
Shrewd Manager	Luke 16:1-18
The Rich Man and Lazarus	Luke 16:19-31
Persistent Widow	Luke 18:1-8
Pharisee and Tax Collector	Luke 18-9-14
Ten Minas	Luke 19:11-27

All Bible references are from the New International Version, unless otherwise indicated.

Each chapter will begin with an explanation of the references in each parable to first-century Palestinian life and the world in which Jesus lived. Then a recounting of each parable will follow. Obviously, no one can retell the parables better than Jesus told them. Interpreting the parables is an attempt to paraphrase, restate, and seek the implications that Jesus intended. In the final sections, each parable is examined for its application to our lives today.

Characteristics

Why are the parables of Jesus so powerful and popular? Several characteristics of his parables offer clues.

1. *The parables of Jesus are essentially oral.* As Jesus told each parable, it came across with great power. This seems to be true partly because the parables are stories. There is something about them that grabs one's attention when someone says to us, "Let me tell you a story." But not everybody can tell a good story.

Certain traits are common to any good story, and the parables of Jesus are no exception. An effective story has a climax, that is, the end of the story carries the main point. Jesus built a parable to its climax, ending it in a different and sometimes surprising way. Another trait of an effective story is its conversational tone. A parable is informal, directed to real people, and lent to ordinary conversation. Jesus told many of his parables in the context of other conversations around a table, in

14

the streets, and in the ordinary places of daily living. A third trait of a good story is its ability to hold the listener's interest and attention. The listener can identify with the point of the story. No wonder the Bible records no instance of his audience going to sleep or of anyone walking out. How could a person walk away from a good story?

2. *The parables of Jesus have a single message.* "Taken altogether," writes Bruce Metzger, "Jesus' parables were governed by a single purpose—to show, directly or indirectly, what God is and what man may become, and to show these things in such a way that they will reach men's hearts if it is possible to reach them at all."[4] This very basic message is at the heart of the parables of Jesus— "The Rule of God" for a person's life.

The parables in this study focus upon the kingdom, the king, and life in the kingdom. Since each parable points to a single message, a parable should not be read as an allegory. In an allegory each person and place is a symbol, pointing to a general or universal truth. But students of the parables have long recognized that "first and most important is the realization that most of the parables have in each one of them one main point and only one."[5] Whenever a parable is confused with an allegory, the interpretation loses its specific, singular quality. Sadly, history offers us numerous examples of such confusion in the twisted interpretations of the parables from the New Testament days to the reformation.[6]

3. *The parables of Jesus can be grouped along certain themes.* The fine volume, *Rediscovering The Parables*, by Joachim Jeremias demonstrates that the para-

bles "fall naturally into groups"; and he suggests ten groups from his own study. My work differs from the work of Jeremias in that it suggests a different set of groups into which the parables may fall. It is not my purpose to treat the parables in the order of their presentation in the gospels. Instead, I want to examine certain key ideas—perspectives on the rule of God—that continually recur in the teachings of Jesus. Each chapter in this book represents a particular group of parables, which focus on a common key idea.

4. *Jesus intersects real life with his parables.* They deal with real needs of real people. They are not fables; there is a certain realism about them. They reveal fresh insights that most people overlook about coins, sheep, nets, trees, banquets, vineyards, treasures, weeds, and other images. These parables carry a message of hope, forgiveness, relationship, meaning, and purpose to humanity. They clearly reveal a God who is interested in the commonplace, the everyday, and the human.

5. *The parables of Jesus are swords that sometimes penetrate the life-styles of people.* Frequently, the parables are "concerned with the situation of conflict—with justification, defense, attack, and even challenge."[7] Far from being merely entertaining stories, the parables of Jesus are sometimes offensive weapons, attacking the life-style and value system of the scribes, the Pharisees, the disciples, or the common people. I see the parables as part of the prophetic, rather than the priestly, tradition of teaching. That is, the point they make confronts the values, morality, and life-styles of those to whom they are directed.

6. *The parables of Jesus are brief.* They seize our attention and hold it. Jesus makes his point quickly before his listener can turn him off. He is in and out in a moment. Some of his parables are but a few sentences in length and can be quickly told. They are vivid, concrete, and even ironic. They are little seed-thoughts ready to germinate. "All experience shows that parables do attract; and when once understood, are sure to be remembered."[8]

7. *The parables of Jesus are permanent.* They are repeatable, enduring. "There is a quality in the parables which time and distance cannot dilute or destroy . . . Many other teachers have told stories that were lively, but he created life."[9] They endure because they deal with truth, not with probabilities or moral contingencies. When we interpret the parables of Jesus, it is crucial to understand the moment or setting in which the parable was first spoken. Jesus delivered them to human beings living in a particular moment in history. What is the chief point that Jesus intends to make? What is the truth that Jesus brings to us? To answer these questions, an understanding of the particular images, appropriate to the first-century Palestinian life setting, that Jesus spoke about to portray the truth about the rule of God is necessary.

8. *Jesus draws his images from daily experience.* He speaks of common, ordinary things, while establishing a new sense of meaning. When he talks about sheep, boys, coins, trees, customs, and plants, he associates the unknown with the known. After having heard a parable, a listener might mentally refer to the fresh, spiritual mean-

ing, which Jesus taught, whenever he encountered the earthly images. Because the images were taken from daily experience, an ancient listener could easily remember the meaning of the parable.

9. *The parables of Jesus are original.* The word "parable" is not, of course, original with Jesus. Greek literary uses of the word predate Jesus several hundred years. They use "parable" in the sense of "a comparison"; literally, "a throwing alongside of." Aristotle counted the parable as a means of demonstration or illustration. That unlike the fable, it takes its material from observation of real life and draws its power from man's ability to see similarities.[10] Jesus never used the parable as a simple comparison or simile, rather he took a basic truth from human life or nature and from it he established a new truth concerning the rule of God for life. The particular content or meaning he gave to a parable is original. None of the parables of Jesus come down to us from sources that existed before him.

10. *The parables of Jesus deal with the mysteries of God.* When the disciples came to Jesus and asked, "Why do you speak to the people in parables?" he replied:

> The knowledge of the secrets of the kingdom of heaven has been given to you, but not to them. Whoever has will be given more, and he will have an abundance. Whoever does not have, even what he has will be taken from him. This is why I speak to them in parables: "Though seeing, they do not see; though hearing, they do not hear or understand."

Matthew 13:10-13

18

When Jesus spoke of the mysteries of God, he referred to them as things that were hidden, known only to God, and revealed by God only at his good pleasure. Jesus imitated a spiritual truth or mystery in the reality of the natural world. So the parables have become God's special instruments of revelation and insight into the spiritual dimension of his rule in the lives of people. They are different from literary productions, speeches, and figures of speech—all of which call attention chiefly to the ingenuity of man.

Another special difference has to do with the particular quality of spiritual truth in the parables. The mystery of God accounts for much of the surprise—or shock—that we find in the endings of the parables.

It's common for a young man to waste his father's wealth and want to return home—but it's unusual to hear of a father who warmly receives such a thoughtless son home.

It's common for a sheep to wander from the flock—but it is unusual for a shepherd to leave the whole flock to search for one sheep.

It is no surprise for a person to incur a large debt—but it is surprising to find a banker who forgives such a sum.

The surprise endings of Jesus' parables challenge us to think in new and different patterns. We can see something we haven't seen before—an insight into the way God works. The surprise and paradox of Jesus' parables can open our hearts to the mysteries of God.

I want to express my special appreciation to Sherry Parsons for her assistance in research and typing the manuscript of this book. I am also deeply indebted to Helen Starnes, my secretary, for her assistance in preparing this book. Finally, I am especially grateful to the people of the South National Church, Springfield, Missouri, for their encouraging response to our studies on the parables.

For nearly two thousand years, men and women have been listening to the parables of Jesus, seeking their meanings, and drawing near to their truths. Let's hope that "seeing we shall perceive, and hearing we will understand." It will challenge the very best that is within us.

Dr. Prentice A. Meador, Jr.
Springfield, Missouri

---

[1] Aristotle, *Poetics*, p. 1459a.

[2] C.H. Dodd, *The Parables of The Kingdom* (New York: Scribner's, 1961), p. 16.

[3] A.M. Hunter, *Interpreting the Parables* (Philadelphia: The Westminister Press, 1960), p. 7.

[4] Bruce M. Metzger, *The New Testament: Its Background, Growth and Content* (Nashville: Abingdon Press, 1965), p. 144.

[5] Walter Russell Bowie, "The Parables," *The Interpreters Bible*, Vol. 7, George A. Buttrick, ed., (New York: Abingdon Press, 1951), p. 173.

[6] Hunter, op. cit., pp. 21-41; Joachim Jeremias, *Rediscovering the Parables* (New York: Charles Scribner's Sons, 1966), pp. 54-70.

[7] Ibid, p. 15.

[8] John M'Clintock and James Strong, *Cyclopaedia of Biblical, Theological and Ecclesiastical Literature*, Vol. 7 (New York: Harper and Brothers, 1891), p. 646.

[9] Bowie, *The Interpreters Bible*, Vol. 7, p. 167.

[10] Aristotle, *Rhetoric*, II, p. 20.

That's The Way God Is 1

Before we can open our lives fully to the rule of God, we need to know as much as we can about who he is and what he is like. Only then can we truly begin to allow him to fill up the emptiness in our own lives, to let him take control of our own hearts.

Because of the presence of Jesus Christ, that is exactly what can happen to us: He is the one who shares with us the mind of God—the concerns, actions, and nature of God. He is the one who helps us construct a picture of God.

Even so, Jesus knows that we are confined to planet earth and, thereby, limited in our ability to understand and know God. That is why Jesus came to a group of people and revealed to them in a unique way who God really is and what he is like. This unique way involved the use of word-pictures, which we call *parables*. To grasp Jesus' teaching about God, we must understand the images Jesus used in revealing God to us.

One place to start is Luke 15, where three different sets of images are found: sheep and shepherds; followed by, coins and lamps; and, then, fathers and sons.

Sheep and Shepherds *(Luke 15:1-7)*

The shepherd in the Palestinian hills and plains grazes his sheep very early in the morning — 4:00 A. M. would not be unusual. As the sun rises, the shepherd leads his flock to green pastures.At midday, he waters his sheep; and by evening, he guides them to a safe place of rest. Psalm 23 portrays the shepherd's care, concern, and duty.

Sheep are timid, docile, animals that are responsive to affection. Because sheep are not good swimmers, they are afraid of rushing waters. They see only a few feet ahead and have no vision of distant objects. As helpless creatures, sheep are utterly defenseless. For sheep to stray is quite common, for they have no sense of direction. Unlike a horse or a dog, who will find his way home when lost, a sheep only seems to wander further away from the flock.

When lost, sheep do not run wildly across creek beds and wilderness plains. They seem to have a lack of initiative, for they lie down and put their legs underneath their bodies. When defenseless and lost, sheep crouch close to the ground.[1]

A shepherd follows an occupation as old as Abel (Gen. 4:2). He is responsible for the welfare of his flock. He must find for them grass and water, protect them against attack, and seek any stray sheep (Ps. 23; Amos 3:12; Ezek. 34:8). It is a common practice for shepherds to give names to their sheep and to call to them at regular intervals, reassuring them of their shepherd's presence. Sheep know their shepherd's voice but may run in the other direction at a stranger's call.

A typical Palestinian shepherd counts his sheep several times during the day and night to be sure that none is lost. Under some circumstances, he must make restitution for sheep he cannot find (Gen. 31:39). Thus, the nature of sheep and the duty of a shepherd make retrieval of the lost a continued necessity.

Leaving his flock with other shepherds, a shepherd will begin a search that may take him through thick brush, into caves, and through streams. When he finds the lost sheep, the shepherd calls to him, runs his hands and arms under the belly of the sheep, and then places him gently on his shoulders. With a sense of satisfaction, he returns the lost one to the flock.[2]

The Lost Sheep (Luke 15:1-7)

Tax collectors, sinners, and others who were the rabble of the land gathered around Jesus. Thus, the religious leaders charged, "You welcome sinners, and you eat with them." In answer, Jesus began to tell a story. Here, in essence, is what he said:

A shepherd had a moderate-sized flock of a hundred sheep. Now, you shepherds know how a flock must be counted at regular intervals. Well, this shepherd found that one of the sheep, one of the unthinking, dependent sheep, had strayed away from the flock. And do you know what he did? He left the flock of ninety-nine and began to

search for the one lost sheep. He looked behind bushes and in caves, calling the name of the sheep. He searched and searched. Then, he saw the sheep—frightened, crouched close to the ground, alone, and defenseless. The shepherd picked him up just as some of you shepherds pick up your lost sheep. He ran his hands and arms under the belly of the sheep, put him over his neck, and carried him on his back. After he had returned to his flock, the shepherd called his friends and neighbors together and said, "I want you to share my good news with me. I lost one of my sheep. I searched, looked, and called. I found him. He was lost, and I found him."

After telling the story, Jesus turned to his accusers. In effect, he told them: "That's what God is like." As sheep, by nature, have trouble comprehending the shepherd, so we have difficulty understanding God and his ways. God searches for straying, unthinking, misguided, and aimless people. His concern leads to an endless search. He finds them and brings them home. Jubilation reigns in his heart when he recovers his lost possession. Yes, that is what God is like—God who lives among men and woman; a God who is diety in the flesh; the Creator who concerns himself over creation.

Coins And Lamps (Luke 15:8-10)

Parables have been called mirrors in which we can see ourselves.[3] This parable centers on a coin, the *drachmē*, which appears only in Luke 15:8 in the New Testament. In American currency, it is equivalent to sixteen cents. One hundred *drachmas* equal the *mina*, and six thousand drachmas make up one *talent*. A *drachmē* equals a day's wage and is the Greek counterpart to a Roman *denarius*.[4] Among the Jews, a woman covered her head with a *kaffiyeh* or head cloth made of substantial material and set with ornaments or jewelry. If she married, coins that constituted her dowry covered the entire front of her head covering.[5] Even today, Palestinian women may be seen wearing a string of coins as a part of their headdress.

Even though a bride may receive many gifts, none of her gifts have the symbolic significance that her headdress of coins has, as this description of Palestinian custom clearly shows:

> She will wear them hooked with little hooks into her hair at the wedding ceremony, and she must guard them with her life thereafter...According to Eastern thinking, if a woman loses one of her ten pieces of silver, God has withdrawn favor from the household, and the blessings which they formerly had have been lost. If she cannot find the coin, she will have to be put out in the street, an outcast; put out to die![6]

Her precious coin must be found! So she lights a lamp, and the search begins.

While lamps are frequently mentioned in the Bible, no description of them appears in scripture. A great variety of lamps for domestic use have been found in Palestine. They are usually made of terra-cotta and bronze. Typically, a household lamp of the Hellenistic period (first century B.C.–A.D.) is like a shallow saucer that holds oil.[7] Jews apparently burned lamps during daylight hours because of the small amount of light entering the door. At night, they burned lamps both to keep away intruders and because of their fear of darkness.

The silver coin may have fallen into a hole in the floor, into a corner, or even beneath dust. Floors in the homes of the rich were typically stone slab, while the poor lived upon floors of beaten clay. Hopefully, a broom would hit the coin and bring it to view. The search could become a long process because, though Palestinian houses were usually small, they were also crowded with furniture, cooking utensils, and clothing.

The Lost Coin (*Luke 15:8-10*)

Jesus again addressed his critics and said, "Let me tell you a story."

A woman had ten silver coins. While in her house one day, she realized that she had lost one of her coins. This neglected coin became the object of her search. She lit a lamp and began to sweep. She swept in the dark corners, in the crevices of the floor, and around the furniture. She swept, hoping that if she hit the coin it would turn up on the floor. But she didn't find it. So she kept searching and sweeping. And, then, she hit it with her broom. She found her coin! And do you know what she did next? She called her friends and neighbors together and said, "You know my dowry, you know how important it is to me. I lost one of my coins, lit a lamp, searched for it, and I found it. That's why I had to share the good news with you.

Jesus then turned to his accusers and in essence said, "That's what God is like." He searches for people who are lonely and lost, for people looking for their identity, and for people out of relationship. God never gives up; and everytime he finds one who is lost, there is great rejoicing in heaven.

Fathers And Sons *(Luke 15:11-32)*

When God first gave Israel their land, they believed that it should remain in the family. Consequently, a basic law of inheritance developed: the family possesses the land, rather than a private individual. Since wills were not known in Judaism before the time of Herod, an inheritance could be received either upon the death of one's father or else by a gift.[8] The law of Moses dictated that the right of inheritance belonged only to the sons of a legal wife (Deut. 21:15-17; Num. 27:8-11). The eldest son would receive a double portion, and the others received equal shares of the estate. Prior to the law of Moses, however, patriarchs would often favor a younger son over the firstborn. Examples include Abraham, Isaac, Jacob, and Joseph.

The younger son could request possession of his share of the estate and turn it into cash. Apparently, this is what happened in Luke 15:11-32.

While living in a foreign culture, the younger son degraded his inheritance, his values, and his religion by working with unclean animals. Leviticus outlined numerous ceremonial defilements that would make purification necessary. Only the ceremonially clean person might approach God in worship (Exod. 19:10; 30:18-21). Having cut himself off from God in worship, the young boy stood in deep need of cleansing. It was common for a

27

person who saw his or her need of cleansing to pray in the manner of David:

> Cleanse me with hyssop, and I will be clean; wash me, and I will be whiter than snow . . . Create in me a pure heart, O God, and renew a steadfast spirit within me . . . A broken and contrite heart, O God, you will not despise.
>
> Psalm 51:7, 10, 17

As a further sign of reconciliation, a Jewish father might kiss his son to restore their relationship (2 Sam. 14:33). "The best robe" would signify an occasion of festivity. More costly than the daily, ordinary robe and usually white in color, this robe might be decorated with jewels or bright scarlet and purple sashes. For the father to present a signet ring would represent a restoration of power and position to the son. If the young boy bared his feet, it would signal his destitution and degradation because sandals were considered the lowliest articles of clothing among the people of Palestine (Mark 1:7). Sandals for his bare feet together with a robe and ring would definitely demonstrate that the father has restored his son to "sonship."

The Lost Boy *(Luke 15:11-32)*

So again Jesus in essence said, "Let me tell you a story."

The younger boy came to his father and said, "Father, I want you to give me my inheritance of your estate today. I don't want to wait any longer. I have big plans, Father. I have places to go and things to do. And I want my share of your property today."

So the father gave the younger son his part of

28

the inheritance. The young man sold it for cash, took his money, and went on a long trip. He began to drink heavily and found some women who thought he was great as long as he could pay for everything.

Inevitably, one day he reached down in his robe and found no more coins! Dead broke, he turned to begging, but since no one would give him anything to eat, the young boy had to begin to feed hogs—a job considered the lowest of the low and a violation of the Sabbath and the law. Now at the point where eating with pigs looked pretty good, he remembered what it was like back home—the joy, the peace, the sense of belonging, the relationship. "I still have a father," he said, "I'll go back home."

So he started the long journey back, which took many days. In walking, he became dirtier and dirtier and began to realize that he simply had no case to present to his father. The young man had already received everything that belonged to him; his father owed him absolutely nothing. Finally, he neared the house where he had been born and raised. He looked up and saw his father running to meet him! When they got home, his father put a robe on his back, a ring on his finger, and sandals on his feet. His father told everyone, "This is my son who has been lost, and today he has come home to me!"

But that's not the end of the story. The older son heard the merriment. He looked in and saw that his rebellious brother had now returned—his brother who had no right to anything, who had taken their father's money and spent it, and who now wore the honorary robe, ring, and sandals. The elder brother stormed up to his father and complained, "I have been with you all this time working and never disobeying an order. I've done everything you asked me to do, and you have never once given me a party. And now this son of yours comes home, and you prepare a calf for him."

One can imagine Jesus, as he came to this part of the story, leaning forward, cupping his hand with his chin in it, and looking directly at his accusers saying, "My son, you are always with me. Everything that belongs to me belongs to you. But we had to celebrate because your brother and my son has come home."

"Whatever a person thinks about God largely determines that person's ministry and mission."

And then Jesus might have told his accusers, "That's what God is like. He is concerned and cares for the rebellious, the selfish, and the totally lost person. And when they respond to God, he will always celebrate!"

The Heart Of God

The earthly ministry of Jesus Christ grounded itself in the nature of God. The Jewish religious leaders thought they had a *prima facie* case in that Jesus was not who he claimed. If he were the Son of God, he would not associate with the unseemly and the rabble of the land. A holy God would associate only with holy people. He would be found at the holy sacrifices in sacred buildings on special days but never with unclean, secular, and needy people.

Jesus did not direct the parables so much to people who knew they were sinners as to the self-righteous and pious. They were the ones who had misunderstood the heart of God. Through the parables of the Lost Sheep, The Lost Coin, and The Lost Boy, Jesus showed that the heart of God is a heart of generosity, love, and compassion. That's the way God is.

Whatever a person thinks about God largely determines that person's ministry and mission. A strong concern for lost people, lonely people, hurting people, and guilty people, issues out of an understanding of a God who is concerned about the real needs of people.

Centuries before Christ, David described God and what He is like: "like a father" (Ps. 103:1-13). For David, any other conception of God missed the point. God is our father! Even when we hurt him, he still loves us. When we reflect badly on his name, he still loves us. When we stray or rebel, still he loves us. He searches, sweeps, and runs to meet us because he is "filled with compassion."

A No-Nonsense God

The way God is often doesn't make much sense to man. At first, it doesn't fit man's logic, his common sense, or his sense of fairness. Rationally, it would follow that a shepherd should stay with the ninety-nine sheep. A woman would take care of the nine coins she has. A father would not be able to accept a boy who rebels against him. That's why "the message of the cross is foolishness to those who are perishing, but to us who are being saved it is the power of God" (1 Cor. 1:18). It didn't make much sense to people in the time of Jesus, so they tried to get themselves off the hook with hairsplitting questions; and finally, they crucified him. If our attitudes of self-satisfaction make us like the Pharisees, the parables of Jesus may not make any more sense to us today than it did to them. But that's the way God is!

"Religion becomes . . . not an experience with God . . . but a series of discussions about God."

It seems too good to be true! We've just never known anyone on earth that has loved us this much, that has ever treated us this way. So many have decided that it really is too good to be true and it can't be true! Religion then becomes for thousands and thousands of people not an experience *with* God, who comes to rule in one's life, but a series of discussions *about* God. So many sincere people, who are lonely and joyless, have never allowed the kingdom to rule in their lives and a loving God to take away their guilt, doubt, and fear. Yet, Jesus still says to us, "That's the way God is!"

What God Can Do

God wants to remove the guilt from our hearts so we can experience his forgiveness. The first step in the story of salvation is God's step. He reaches out to us. In our response, we bring to God a humble and contrite heart (Ps. 51). God wants to release people from the memory, the guilt, and the regret of past sins. God wants people to experience freedom and release from a life of misdirection, worry, neglect, and rebellion.

The thread that runs throughout the Scripture is that man is to bring to God a willing and humble heart. No more evasion, no more blaming of circumstances, and no more claim of ignorance. We bring only a sense of personal accountability and a willingness to receive God's total forgiveness. Only then can we feel a renovated spirit, a cleaned heart, and a feeling of forgiveness.

The experience of forgiveness allows us to affirm our salvation in Jesus, to forgive other people, and to discover our own gifts or talents that can become our ministries. A life of celebration and worship, service to others, and deep, personal peace will characterize the life of the forgiven. We would then know how it feels to be a sheep who has been brought back to the flock, a coin who has been found, and a boy who has returned to his father. We would know how it feels to be made whole after living broken lives. We would know how it feels to replace holiness with intimate friendship with God.

What is your conception of God? Do you think he is enjoying your misery? angry at your rebellion? punishing you through your pain? Do you think he satisfies his needs at your expense?

Or, do you see that he satisfies *your* needs at *his* expense (John 3:16)? Do you see God as flowing with forgiving compassion? Do you see that he is the only hope of the hopeless, the despairing, and the totally lost!

"This man welcomes sinners and eats with them," was the accusation of the Pharisees and the teachers of the law (Luke 15:2). But Jesus responded that there was a reason why he gathered sinners into his community. There was a reason why caring and sharing would be the main function of the church. There was a reason why man's deepest needs would be fulfilled in Christ.

It's because "That's the way God is."

---

[1] For background information on sheep, see J.D. Douglas, ed., *The New Bible Dictionary* (Grand Rapids: Eerdmans Publishing Co., 1975), p. 1174; Merrill C. Tenney, ed., *The Zondervan Pictorial Bible Dictionary* (Grand Rapids: Zondervan Publishing House, 1963), p. 44.

[2] For additional reading on shepherds, note Joachim Jeremias, *Rediscovering the Parables* (New York: Charles Scribner's Sons, 1966), pp. 105-106.

[3] Archibald M. Hunter, *Interpreting the Parables* (Philadelphia: The Westminster Press, 1960), p. 10.

[4] Douglas, op. cit., p. 840.

[5] Tenney, op. cit., p. 227.

[6] K.C. Pillai, *Light Through An Eastern Window* (New York: Robert Speller and Sons, 1963), pp. 6-7.

[7] Tenney, op. cit., p. 475.

[8] Douglas, op. cit., p. 562; Jeremias, op. cit., pp. 101-102.

There's A New Day Coming 2

For all too many people today, life seems brutal, lonely, and meaningless. Millions have agreed with Ernest Hemingway that an early death should be considered a choice blessing. In his classic novel, *A Farewell To Arms*, Hemingway wrote:

> The world breaks everyone . . . Those that will not break it kills. It kills the very good and the very gentle and the very brave impartially. If you are none of these you may be sure that it will kill you too, but there will be no special hurry.[1]

Fortunate is the person, according to Hemingway, who does not have to live life and discover its brutality, guilt, and loneliness.[2]

But is there ever a chance for a new beginning in life? Is there ever an opportunity for a fresh start? Can there be a New Day? Is there ever a time when the sun dispels the darkness of loneliness, fear, guilt, and hurt? Is there any option to being broken by life or an early death? Is life totally absurd; or, can it have purpose, direction, and meaning?

For the Christian, Jesus steps in at the point of these questions and offers God's way for a person's life. He assures us that we can find the divine authority by which to guide our lives. Through Christ, we can find the knowledge and the spiritual power to fill the blankness inside us. Jesus offers us God's rule for life in the place of self-rule. Making God's rule possible was the central purpose in Jesus' earthly life:

> The Spirit of the Lord is on me, because, he has anointed me to preach good news to the poor. He has sent me to proclaim freedom for the prisoners and recovery of sight for the blind, to release the oppressed, to proclaim the year of the Lord's favor.
>
> Luke 4:18-19

Jesus offered an option to a hopeless and lonely world. He made a grand announcement in the symbolic language of parables. Through word-pictures of fig trees, wineskins, and banquets, Jesus made his declaration: "There's a New Day coming!"

Fig Trees   *(Matt. 24:32-35;   Mark 18:28-32; Luke 21:29-33)*

Ancient people considered fig trees symbols of prosperity, peace, and triumph. In Latin mythology, Bacchus held the fig tree to be sacred and employed it in numerous religious ceremonies. The Romans considered the fig tree to be their chief symbol for the future prosperity of Rome.

The Old Testament frequently refers to the fig tree. Jews regarded figs "so valuable, that to cut them down if they yielded even a small measure of fruit was popularly deemed to deserve death at the hand of God."[3] Ancient Israel considered figs a special attraction in the promised land, which they described as "a land of wheat and barley, vines and fig trees, pomegranates . . . " (Deut. 8:8). In order to show the great prosperity of Palestine, the spies brought back figs to show the tribes (Num. 13:23). When Israel wanted to describe the desolation and poverty of the wilderness, they described it as a place with "no grain or figs, grapevines or pomegranates . . . " (Num. 20:5). To show the future prosperity of Israel, the prophet Joel used the fig tree as an emblem when he wrote " . . . for the open pastures are becoming green. The trees are bearing their fruit; the fig tree and the vine yield their riches" (Joel 2:22). "Almost all the references to the fruit of the fig tree," writes one interpreter, "are indications of its great importance to the life of ancient times, as it continues to be in the Holy Land today."[4]

Before fig trees yielded a bumper crop, years of patient care needed to pass. Passage of time is integral to our understanding of the parable of Luke 13:6-9. Jews regarded the fig tree as the most fruitful of all trees. They gave it the favored place in the vineyard.[5] Even today, throughout the winter the fig trees of the Holy Land remain bare until the beginning of spring. Then a remarkable process takes place. Unlike many of the other trees of Palestine, the fig tree appears to be dead with its bare branches, but it begins to bloom small leaf buds and, *at the same time,* tiny figs begin to appear in the leaf axils. These early signs of spring herald new life, a new time of the year.[6]

The Budding Fig Tree *(Matt. 24:32-35; Mark 13:28-32; Luke 21:29-33)*

Jesus declared in each of these parables that the time for the rule of God in the hearts and lives of people had come. The prophets had yearned for this long awaited New Day and had predicted its coming. But when is this New Day coming? To some students of the Bible, the context in which this parable was told seems to point to the second coming of Christ. But others believe that these parables point to the coming of the kingdom of God. Thus, Jesus would be announcing the New Day of the rule of God, the day of salvation. And he does so by saying in effect once more, "Let me tell you a story."

Throughout the winter, the fig tree sheds all its leaves, remains bare, and gives every appearance of deadness. But have you noticed that as winter turns to spring, its twigs become tender and it blossoms tender green leaves. Even though it appears to have been dead, the fig tree gives every appearance of life. Winter is over, and summer is near.

Then, Jesus turned to his disciples and his enemies and in essence said, "That's the way the rule of God can be in a person's life. It is near." Evidences of deadness appear in every person's life: the guilt, the loneliness, the confusion, the meaninglessness, the confusion, and the insensitivity to others. But Jesus announced that a New Day was coming! The winter of the old covenant now gives way to the summer of God's salvation. The rule of God in the lives of individuals is close at hand! Jesus has come! There is hope!

Garments and Wine *(Matt. 9:16-17; Mark 2:21-22; Luke 5:36-38)*

It was a necessity for the poor to repair a worn robe, rather than to buy a new one. In order to repair a torn old garment, cloth needed to be "dressed" or shrunk to prevent further tearing. It is possible that Jesus may have watched his mother mend threadbare garments using this exact technique.[7]

The reference "new wine" referred to wine made "from the first drippings of the juice before the winepress was trodden. As such it would be particularly potent."[8] Jews placed new wine in a new goatskin pouch (Josh. 9:4, 13). A new leather pouch would be pliable and flexible enough to expand with the fermenting new wine. But new wine in a cracked, hard, and old wineskin would burst the skin. New wine required a fresh wineskin.[9]

New Garment, New Wineskin *(Matt. 9:16-17; Mark 2:21-22; Luke 5:36-38)*

When Jesus was challenged by John's disciples as to why his disciples did not fast, he heard a deeper question which challenged his authority to announce a New Day. Perhaps change frightened his questioners or maybe they had become comfortable in their traditions. In responding to the challenge, Jesus told his hearers a story. Here in essence is what he said:

You know how a woman patches an old garment! She does not take a new patch and sew it on an old garment. If she did, there would be shrinking and tearing.

You have seen how men pour new wine into wineskins. They put the new wine in a new wineskin so that when the fermentation begins the wineskin will expand. If they place the new wine in a stretched, cracked, and old wineskin, it would burst. The wine and wineskin would be lost.

Then, Jesus turned to his inquirers and said in effect, "That's the way it is with the kingdom of God. There's a New Day coming!" The old garment and the old wineskin may point to either worn-out Judaism with its threadbare forms and traditions or to a person's hardened, inflexible heart. The new garment and the new wine signal a New Day, a fresh direction for the lives of people. He invited all to wear the new garment! All are invited to drink the new wine! Here, then, is the heart of the good news: "Therefore, if anyone is in Christ, he is a new creation; the old has gone, the new has come!" (2 Cor. 5:17).

Banquets *(Luke 14:15-24)*

Banquets played an important part in weddings throughout Palestine. A marriage ceremony would usually last ten days, and all the neighbors would be invited to celebrate. If any of them were engaged in fasting and prayer, they would be called upon to suspend such activities for the duration of the marriage feast, for they believed

God to be present at the marriage ceremony. Jesus referred to this custom in Matthew 9:15 when he said, "How can the guests of the bridegroom mourn while he is with them? The time will come when the bridegroom will be taken from them; then they will fast." "These guests," writes one scholar, "observed the custom of suspending prayer and fasting during the marriage ceremony period; but when this is completed, they may then resume any prayers or fasting they had in progress."[10]

Banquets in biblical times were sumptuous festivals. Amos painted a striking portrait of the typical banquet: guests recline on beds of ivory; they eat lambs and calves; they drink wine and sing songs; they anoint themselves with oil (Amos 6:4-6). Even though the consumption of rich foods constituted a chief feature of the banquet in biblical times, in Roman banquets consumption for the sake of consumption took over. For example, Petronius describes in rich and explicit detail Roman banquets in his *Satyricon*. Jewish banquets, in contrast, were normally a part of religious or family ceremonies.

A feast occupied center stage in other celebrations, in addition to celebrations of marriage. Such a feast was for sacrifices (Exod. 34:15; Judg. 16:23-25), birthdays (Gen. 40:20; Job 1:4; Matt. 14:6), funerals (Jer. 16:7), the laying of foundations for buildings (Prov. 9:1-5), sheep-shearing (1 Sam. 25:2, 36), and wine harvesting (Judg. 9:27). "A banquet always included wine drinking; it was not simply a feast in our sense."[11] A great feast would last for several days. However, excessive eating and drinking (Isa. 5:11 f) was condemned in the Old Testament.

A great banquet would draw great ceremony, attention, and celebration. The host of the banquet would invite all of his guests a considerable time before the banquet. Then, on the day and at the hour of the banquet, he would send one or more of his servants to the expected guests with the announcement that the preparations for the feast were complete and that their presence was expected. The second invitation was delivered verbally by the messenger in his master's name. (It is important to recognize that the master sent his second invitation only to those who had already been invited and declared acceptable.) Any action other than acceptance was considered rejection not only of the feast but of the host as well: "People are bound by every feeling of honor and propriety to postpone all other engagements to the duty of waiting upon their entertainer."[12] When the host completed his preparations for the great banquet, he would send forth the invitation: "Everything is ready . . . come to the wedding banquet" (Matt. 22:4).

The Great Banquet (Luke 14:15-24)

Crucial events provided the setting for the great banquet story. A very prominent Pharisee invited Jesus, along with other selected guests, to eat at a feast in his home. By this point in his ministry, Jesus had already confronted the prevalent attitude of Phariseeism. As a result, they "carefully watched him." The Pharisees and experts in the law of Moses tried to find reasons to disprove his claim. They placed him under their religious magnifying glass looking for evidence to confirm that he was not the Son of God. Their judgmental actions turned the dinner into a trial. But this time the issue was not a written code but a human being—"a man suffering from dropsy." It would seem unlikely that the prominent Pharisee would have invited such an embarrassing person to his great feast. But he came. Everyone could see him, but who would respond to his need on the Sabbath day? Totally unable to coordinate his body and falling in front of all the prominent and the wealthy, the poor man appeared foolish!

The great magnitude of human need moved the compassionate heart of God. Jesus healed the man and sent him out of the room. Then, Jesus asked the lawyers and Pharisees a question: "Suppose your ox or son fell in a well on the wrong day, on the Sabbath day. Will you not pull him out?" Silence blanketed the feast, a cold, quiet response to Jesus' question. Jesus looked at the arrangement of the prominent, upstanding, and sophisticated guests seated around the feast table. The wealthy with their robes, jewelry, and turbans sat next to the prominent, who had their credentials of self-importance. Such people shunned people with dropsy. Jesus listened as they talked about whom they knew, how much they owned, and how wise they had become. All around the table, the self-righteous mingled with the pious, the sophisticated mixed with the proud. Out of step with the table talk, Jesus addressed the self-deceived: "When you were invited to a wedding feast, do not sit in the place of honor. Take the lowest place. For everyone who exalts himself will be humbled, and he who humbles himself will be exalted."

To his now uncomfortable, prominent host, Jesus gave the mark of true spirituality: "When you give a feast, invite the poor, the crippled, the lame, and the blind; and you will be blessed. Invite those who cannot repay you, and you will be repaid at the resurrection of the righteous."

One self-righteous guest heard Jesus and then piously claimed to be on God's side: "What a great blessing it will be to enter into God's messianic kingdom and to accept it." Jesus, knowing that none of those around the table grasped the nature of the rule of God in a person's life, in essence replied, "Let me tell you a story."

A man announced a great banquet and invited many of his close, personal friends, including the prominent, the landowners, the wealthy, and the sophisticated. Then, he began extensive preparations for the feast according to the proper customs:

* prepared the meal and selected the choice wines
* secured new and costly robes for his guests as a token of his personal esteem and appreciation
* arranged for the seating of the honored around his table
* secured the finest oil for anointing the guests, their robes, and their beards
* gathered the most beautiful garlands for decoration
* prepared the music, the singing, and the dancing

44

So the preparations were the finest, and the feast was ready.

According to custom, the host sent his servant to announce, "Come, everything is now ready for the feast." As the master's servant gave this second invitation to a guest, he listened to the response, "I can't come. I'm just too busy in my business to attend the feast. I just bought a new field to go with my other fields. And I really need to spend that time in looking at my new purchase. Please ask your master to excuse me."

So the master's servant went to another already invited guest and invited him again. But the guest said, "I can't come. I'm too overwhelmed with my work. I just bought oxen to go with my other flocks and herds. I need to find out how strong and hardworking my oxen are. Tell your master I would really like to come, but I can't."

So the servant continued to go from guest to guest announcing, for the second time, his master's great banquet. Another guest told him, "I just can't come. You see my wife and I just married and we're in love. We just can't break away from each other. There's no way that I can attend the feast and take the time to be at the banquet. Please excuse me."

So the servant went back to his master and with his head down reported, "Not a guest is coming! Not one of the people you invited will be here. When you serve dinner, there will not be anyone at the table."

The owner of the house then became angry and instead of inviting the powerful, the rich, the influential, and all of those who are successful, he ordered his servant to invite people like the man with the dropsy. "Go out quickly into the streets and alleys of the town and bring in the hurting, the lame, the lonely, the guilty, the blind, the prostitutes, and the 'not-so-good people' of the land. Go out to the road and country lanes and make them come in so that my house will be full. I tell you, not one of those men who were invited will get a taste of my banquet."

As Jesus told this parable to the people gathered around the Pharisee's table, one can imagine an embarrassed silence settling over them. For Jesus in effect told them, "Here is the way the rule of God is." It is like a banquet feast that has been prepared for thousands of years for people like you. My master invited you, but your narrow-minded, stubborn, materialistic and self-righteous ways have kept you from the banquet table. So now I'm going to invite the uninvited—the guiltridden, the lonely, the depressed, the poor, and the foolish. There's a New Day coming!

The God Who Acts

The Old Testament is filled with hope of a New Day coming. Some seven hundred and fifty years before Jesus spoke the parables Isaiah described a New Day:

> Then will the eyes of the blind be opened and the ears of the deaf unstopped. Then will the lame leap like a deer, and the tongue of the dumb shout for joy. Water will gush forth in the wilderness and streams in the desert. The burning sand will become a pool, the thirsty ground bubbling springs.
>
> Isaiah 35:5-7a

The prophetic word is but one Old Testament tributary constantly flowing into the stream of the kingdom of God. The belief and hope that God would act in history, that a New Day was coming, and that a Messianic age is in the future had their origins in the headwaters of the covenant with Abraham (Gen. 12:1-3). The Mosaic covenant and the beliefs of the nation of Israel continued to feed the stream of hope that God would act in history. Later, in the years of captivity and religious apostasy, the stream would be reduced to only a small trickle in the parched desert.

On the pages of the New Testament, the stream of hope and expectation becomes a mighty, rushing torrent. "But when the time had fully come, God sent his Son . . . " (Gal. 4:4). The New Testament centers in the new here-and-now activity of God. "For God so loved the world that he gave his one and only Son . . . " (John 3:16). The New Testament should not be thought of as a book about some new ethic, new religion, or new view of God and man. As John Bright has pointed out, "Jesus did not announce to the Jews that a loftier notion of God was now available—but that their God had acted!"[13] This does not undercut the supremacy of the New Testament to the Old, but it is a mistake to set the New Testament *against* the Old. The New Testament declares that the God of creation and history "became flesh and lived for a little while among us" (John 1:14). God, whose activity was longed for, hoped for, and prayed for, has acted decisively in Jesus Christ. This is the message of the parables. At last, the summer of God's salvation is here. His long awaited banquet is now being served. It is time to put on the new garments and get on with the celebration!

The Call of Jesus

The New Testament heralds Jesus of Nazareth to be the grand, climatic activity of God. Before the coming of Jesus, the kingdom of God was described in future tense. Jesus changed the tense of the rule of God to the present. For example, early in his Galilean ministry, Jesus announced a New Day: "The time has come. The kingdom of God is near. Repent and believe the good news!" (Mark 1:15). Immediately, Jesus began to call men to him in order that God might rule their hearts.

"Jesus changed the tense of the rule of God to the present."

Some who answered the call of Jesus, however, misread him. They looked for a political kingdom, a government more powerful than Rome that would be able to rule the world by Jesus' leadership. Even as Jesus spoke of "the kingdom of God," they cast his ideas in political terms. Consequently, many misunderstood the nature of God's rule. As they increased their opposition toward Jesus, they understood less and less of his parables. He began to reserve the deep meaning of his parables for those who already had committed themselves to him. Even today, if we try to understand the kingdom of God in any sense other than the one he gave us, then we, too, will miss the deep meaning! What is required is openness of heart and humility of spirit. With this beginning, our understanding of the rule of God and its special nature will become clear and evident.

Inside Out

All of us have experienced guilt, loneliness, confusion, and fear. None of us can live without personal worth, security, affirmation, and love. Yet, unless God has acted on our behalf, life becomes a random collection of happenings. Ugliness and meaninglessness become the norm. Our choices narrow down to one: a life with no hope. We feel totally controlled by circumstances.

"God does not seek to "scotch-tape" blessings to my life but stands ready to completely fill my life inside out."

What a contrast is the message of the gospel! "There's a New Day coming." A new thing has happened—God has acted! And he has acted for *me*. He wants to bring meaning to my life. God does not seek to "scotch-tape" blessings to my life but stands ready to completely fill my life inside out. "Here I am! I stand at the door and knock. If anyone hears my voice and opens the door, I will go in and eat with him, and he with me" (Rev. 3:20).

Here at Thy table, Lord, This sacred hour;
O let us feel Thee near, In loving pow'r;
Calling our thoughts away From self and sin,
As to Thy banquet hall We enter in.

Sit at the feast, dear Lord, Break Thou the bread;
Fill Thou the cup that brings Life to the dead;
That we may find in Thee, Pardon and peace;
And from all bondage win A full release.

So shall our life of faith Be full, be sweet;
And we shall find our strength For each day
   meet:
Fed by Thy living bread, All hunger past,
We shall be satisfied, And saved at last.

Come then, O Holy Christ, Feed us, we pray;
Tough with Thy pierced hand Each common day;
Making this earthly life Full of Thy grace,
Till in the home of hea'v We find our place.

William F. Sherwin

---

[1] Ernest Hemingway, *A Farewell To Arms* (New York: Scribner, 1940), p. 249.

[2] Carlos Baker, *Ernest Hemingway: A Life Story* (New York: Scribner, 1969), p. 271.

[3] Alfred Edersheim, *The Life and Times of Jesus The Messiah*, Vol. 2 (Grand Rapids: William B. Eerdmans Publishing Co., 1953), p. 246.

[4] J.C. Trever, "Fig Tree," *The Interpreter's Dictionary of the Bible*, Vol. 2 (Nashville: Abingdon Press, 1962), p. 267.

[5] Edersheim, *Op. Cit.*, p. 247.

[6] For further background on fig trees, read E.W. Masterman, "Fig, Fig-Tree," *International Standard Bible Encyclopedia*, Vol. 2, pp 1108-1109; Joachim Jeremias, *Rediscovering the Parables* (New York: Charles Scribner's Sons, 1966), pp. 93-94.

[7] George A. Buttrick, *The Parables of Jesus* (New York: Harper & Brothers, 1928), p. 6.

[8] F.S. Fitzsimmonds, "Wine and Strong Drink," *The New Bible Dictionary* (Grand Rapids: William B. Eerdman's Publishing Co., 1975), p. 1331.

[9] Arthur B. Fowler, "Bottle," *The Zondervan Pictorial Bible Dictionary* (Grand Rapids: Zondervan Publishing House, 1963), p. 130; Edersheim, *The Life and Times of Jesus the Messiah*, Vol. 1, p. 665.

[10] K.C. Pillai, *Light Through An Eastern Window* (New York:

Speller & Sons, 1963), pp. 8-9.

[11] Steven Barabas, "Banquet," *The Zondervan Pictorial Bible Dictionary*, p. 95.

[12] John M'Clintock and James Strong, "Banquet," *Cyclopaedia of Biblical, Theological and Ecclesiastical Literature*, Vol. 1 (New York: Harper & Brothers, 1891), p. 635.

[13] John Bright, *The Kingdom of God* (Nashville: Abingdon Press, 1953), p. 195.

Don't Overlook Tiny Beginnings 3

Each year when new cars hit the market, car makers appeal to the public to pay close attention to the latest features: a smooth running engine, luxurious options, and comfortable riding. One phrase we hear over and over, year after year, is "engineering miracle."

Suppose, however, that the automakers announced a new, expensive, and smooth-running sports car! After years of plans and drawing boards, the new model rolls off the assembly line. But the ads and commercials tell you that the sleek sports car was made from a bent fender, a rusty bumper, broken screws, a burned-out headlamp, a half-used battery, a high-mileaged transmission, and some treadless tires! To develop a fine automobile from such materials—now that would be an "engineering miracle"!

Now, suppose instead that you were going to start a worldwide religion. You could start with big money, a big city, and big people. The religion of Sun Moon got started that way. Or, you could start with no money, a small, troubled country, and people nobody ever heard of. You know, of course, who was able to build a worldwide religion from four fishermen, several tax collectors, a political revolutionist, several prostitutes, and average people who had no money, no contacts, no wealth, nor knowledge. It certainly made no logical sense that a worldwide religion could begin with such humble materials. And you could call that a true "engineering miracle."

In the way he drew followers, Jesus revealed a truth about the rule of God in the lives of people. This fundamental truth emerged in a group of parables. To understand and appreciate his message meant looking beyond what met the eye and listening for more than what was said to the ear.

This is why I speak to them in parables:
Though seeing, they do not' see;
    though hearing, they do not hear or under-
    stand.
In them is fulfilled the prophecy of Isaiah:
You will be ever hearing but never understand-
    ing;
you will be ever seeing but never perceiving.

Matthew 13:13-14

So, at first, the rule of God makes no rational sense to human beings. Eventually, however, we can come to see from the parables of Jesus who God really is and how he works with us and in us.

Mustard Seed And Leaven

Jewish rabbis used the phrase "small as a mustard seed" as a proverb to refer to the very smallest amount, remnant, or residue.[1] So our Lord's phrase "faith as small as a mustard seed" (Matt. 17:20; Luke 17:6) communicated clearly to the people of his day the tiniest germ of faith.

In biblical times, several types of mustard had extraordinarily tiny seeds. Sometimes today we see necklaces and other pieces of jewelry that are made with mustard seeds. Even so, as one writer explained, "the seeds of the East are really about one-tenth of the size of the ones that grow in America and Europe. They are truly the smallest of seeds, and the plants they produce grow as large as trees."[2] The pinhead size of a mustard seed, ". . . The smallest seed you plant in the ground" (Mark 4:31) distinguished it from other Palestinian seeds. Under favorable conditions, a mustard seed would grow into a very tall shrub tree, reaching ten to twelve feet in height. ". . . It grows and becomes the largest of all garden plants, with such big branches that the birds of the air can perch in its shade" (Mark 4:32).[3]

Bread constituted an important part of the diet of the people of Palestine. Breadmaking is an ancient and relatively simple process. A Jewish woman would mix flour with water and salt and knead the dough in a special trough. In order to bake leavened bread, she would add a piece of dough "retained from a former baking, which had fermented and turned acid."[4] She either dissolved the leaven in water in the trough before she added flour or submerged the leaven in the flour and continued to knead it. She customarily covered the dough with a cloth and left it to stand over night. By morning, the leaven had assimilated throughout the whole dough. Its lively chemical action dynamically penetrated the entire mass. She would complete the process by baking the dough either over hot stones or in a oven. People today who study this ancient process of bread-making know of no other sort of leaven, although it has been suggested that the Jews also used the lees of wine for yeast.[5]

Leaven has two kinds of symbolic significance in the Bible. On one hand, the scripture may describe leaven as a symbol of corruption. The capacity of leaven for spreading its fermenting power throughout the whole mass of dough may be inferred from Old Testament passages and is clearly indicated in the New Testament. For example, Jesus warned against the "leaven" of the Pharisees and the Sadducees (Matt. 16:11). Paul cautioned against a little moral corruption throwing an entire church into moral confusion (1 Cor. 5:6-8). "A little yeast works through the whole batch of dough," he wrote to the churches of Galatia (Gal. 5:9). In another kind of symbolism, however, leaven stands for the positive process of moral influence. When Jesus likened the growth of the kingdom of God among people to the pervasive working of the yeast, he used "leaven" as a symbol for spiritual development.[6]

The Mustard Seed And The Leaven
(Matt.13:31-33; Luke 13:18-21)

Crowds of curious, hurting, and lonely people

often gathered around Jesus. On one occasion, he told this little story:

A man took the tinest of all seeds, a mustard seed, and planted it in his field. After weeks and months of growing, the man found that this tiny seed had grown into a tall mustard tree with birds in its branches.

Then, Jesus turned to the crowd and said in effect, "That's the way the rule of God works." God plants his rule in the fields of the world. It is a tiny beginning and easily overlooked. He begins with totally lost people, common people, in a far-off corner of the earth. Yet, even though its origin is so small, its end is so great! God's rule among the people is destined to move among the ethnic groups of the whole earth. It includes men and women, Jews and Gentiles, all races, all languages, and all nations. What a magnificent contrast: from a tiny beginning to the greatest ending! Guilty, hurting, and lonely people become God's redeemed for all ages.

After speaking about the mustard seed, Jesus told the crowd of followers another story:

You know how a woman bakes bread. Before going to bed at night, she takes time to begin preparation for a large amount of bread. On one occasion, a woman was planning to make enough bread to feed more than a hundred people. She took a scrap of leaven and placed it into a bushel of dough. She then worked the leaven into the whole batch of dough. Because it was such a large amount, she continued to knead the dough until she worked it throughout the batch.

She then covered the dough and retired for the evening. She awoke to find that the leaven had moved through the whole batch. Swollen and larger, the dough showed that the leaven had worked through it during the night.

Then, Jesus turned to the crowd and in essence said, "That is the way the rule of God works." Like leaven, the kingdom of God begins with a tiny, almost unnoticeable beginning. But when a person receives the reign of God, it starts to work at once—quietly, powerfully, dynamically, gradually pervading the whole of one's life. One mark of the kingdom of God is its flourishing growth and boundless vitality. God challenges a person's sense of values, purpose, and relationships. His rule provides a radically new reason for living. His rule among us may bring persecution, intimidation, apathy, or curiosity. But one thing is always true of the growth of the kingdom of God— nothing can stop it!

Seed Time To Harvest

Because of the rain cycle, seed time for ancient Palestinian farmers usually fell in late November or December. A farmer might either sow seed and plow it under the ground or plow the ground first and then sow the seed. In either case, the seed was scattered broadcast. At times, farmers used cattle to tread the seed into the soil.

In the latter case, a sack with holes was filled with corn and layed on the back of the animal, so that, as it moved onwards, the seed was thickly scattered. Thus it might well be, that it would fall indiscriminately on beaten roadway, on stony places but thinly covered with soil, or where the thorns had not been cleared away, or undergrowth from the thorn-hedge crept into the field, as well as on good ground.[7]

In the Old Testament, farming that employed anything other than fertile, rich soil was considered ineffective farming (Job 5:6; Prov. 24:30-32). The productivity of the crop depended in great measure on the amount of rainfall during the next several months. Heavy winter rains usually gave the crops enough moisture, but the rains of March and April were needed to bring the grain to harvest.[8]

Harvest marked the end of the growing season, a time for gathering in the fruits of labor. In Palestine it usually fell during the middle of April, following the spring rains. The Old Testament descriptions state that harvest began with the barley and ended with the wheat and with the Feast of the Passover (Lev. 23:9-14; 2 Sam. 21:9-10). The most thorough Old Testament explanation of harvest is found in Ruth 2 and 3. Here we read that workers collected the sheaves into a heap or removed them to threshing floors. Unmuzzled oxen trod upon the grain, separating the chaff and the straw from the grain. By use of a fan and with the help of the wind, a harvester would winnow the grain. The remaining grain would be placed in storage bins.[9] Palestinian farmers considered 10 percent to be a good harvest. In comparison, 30, 60, and 100 percent symbolized an unusual bounty.[10]

The Sower *(Matt. 13:3-8; Mark 4:3-8; Luke 8:5-8)*

Feeling the pressure of the large crowds who

had come to him, Jesus got into a boat and continued to teach—this time with yet another story.

Once a farmer began to broadcast his seed. Some of the seed fell out where the birds could eat it. Other seed fell on the path alongside the field, where the sun could scorch it. Some seed fell among rocks and even among thorns. But do you know what happened to some of the other seed? It fell into rich, fertile earth.

After a number of months of rain and patient waiting, the small seed began to produce a huge crop. Some of the harvest turned out to be thirty times larger than the seed. Some was fifty times larger than the seed, and some even a hundred times larger.

Then Jesus explained to the large crowds, "That's the way the rule of God is in the hearts and lives of people." Even the tiniest seed, which God plants, produces a bountiful harvest. The ways of God are sometimes unnoticeable, quiet, and undramatic. According to the standards of men, who look for every great event to be accompanied by sound and fury, the rule of God in the life of people may receive no serious notice. But God nourishes that seed and brings about a harvest that surpasses all human expectations and measures. It's a tiny beginning, but take care not to overlook it.

The Patient Farmer (Mark 4:26-29)

Then, how long does it take for the kingdom of God to grow? When will the harvest be? These questions in particular seem to haunt the disciples of Jesus. In their understanding of the nature of the kingdom, it would begin with a political revolution during their lifetime. But there were those who had been awaiting the coming of God's kingdom for years and had leaned upon the Old Testament prediction of the coming of the kingdom. In answering all those who were looking for the kingdom, Jesus told this story:

A farmer broadcasts seed on his fertile land. Nourished by rain and fed by the soil, the seed grows during the night and day. Whether the farmer wakes in the night to check his crop or whether he sleeps through the night, the seed continues to grow. The seed spontaneously produces the stalk, then the head, and then the full kernel ready for harvest. When the harvest time comes, the farmer cuts down his crop. Even as he cuts down the harvest, he does not understand how the seed sprouted into the full kernel.

Again, Jesus' point was the same: "That's the way the rule of God is in the hearts of people." God's mission to earth is to sow the seed of "good news" in the lives of people. Regardless of circumstances or conditions, God's seed quietly grows to harvest. People can do nothing about the working of God except to wait patiently for it. As God releases his divine plan into the world, people are to allow it to grow into its own harvest. How long will it take? That question is answered in God's own time frame. The task of man is to be patient. In faith, God's people join God in his mission and believe with confidence and assurance that he will bring his mission to fulfillment.

Tiny Beginnings And Triumphant Ends

Too often we suffer from the activist delusion that nothing significant happens unless it is accompanied by a loud noise. When we listen to tv ads, we may notice that the volume is usually increased to get the viewer's attention. We are tempted to believe that noise and news go together. According to human standards, anything which begins with significance must be accompanied with neon lights, fireworks, and spotlights. How different is the wisdom of God! He works in almost unnoticeable ways.

"If we only look for God in religious settings . . . we will miss many of the quiet, tiny, yet highly significant works of Christ in our lives."

Remember that God's Son was born in a manger! This simplicity bothers some people who have difficulty in realizing that God is at home in a humble address. We sometimes think that if we could change the routine of our lives, God would be more real to us. But God works through the routine of our lives, in the ordinary details of daily living. His power turns an average Thursday into a day of triumph. If we only look for God in religious settings and on religious days, we will miss many of the quiet, tiny, yet highly significant works of Christ in our lives—even as some missed his birth.

Following the birth of Jesus, no one would have dreamed that the life and ministry of the carpenter's son would herald a new day of God. John Bright writes of this very truth in his excellent volume *The Kingdom of God:*

> The kingdom of God, then, is a power already released in the world. True, its beginnings are tiny, and it might seem incredible that the humble ministry of this obscure Galilean could be the dawning of the new age of God. Yet it is! What has been begun here will surely go on to its conclusion; nothing can stop it. And the conclusion is victory.[11]

Consider those that Jesus called to be his apostles! For the most part, they were men without credentials, small in number, and without much prospect for the future. And they seemed to miss the point about the business of the kingdom. But God's power turned this small group of unknown men into the beginning of the Christian faith, which has spread through the nations of the earth. God started where he found them, never gave up on them, and used them to continue his work.

Consider, for instance, the way in which God began his church! Looking back, give a great deal of attention to the day of Pentecost and the events of Acts 2. But the Roman world apparently was not even aware that it took place. From their standpoint the church had a tiny beginning— easily overlooked and considered an insignificant event in history. The Romans would not have placed the events of Acts 2 in the top ten news events of the year. But God worked through insignificant beginnings to bring ends of triumph. And his church has endured long past the Roman Empire.

An Important Principle

Today God calls upon his people to use the same spiritual principle that he uses. In the tiny beginnings of our daily living, God brings about great results. For example, when a father and mother pray nightly with their children, it may seem like the tiniest of events. Or when a family gathers on family night and studies the Bible, prays, and talks about God, it may seem a small affair. But this is God's way of raising up future leaders of his church. Teaching a group of children every Sunday morning may seem like an unnoticed event. But this is God's way of developing committed missionaries, dedicated husbands and wives, and full-time devoted workers.

"He calls upon his church to see the validity of this important spiritual principle: the infinitely great can be seen in the infinitely small."

Again, God calls upon his people to render acts of service, however small and insignificant they may seem. Who would ever dream that an encouraging word given to a prisoner or to a sick person might ultimately lead them to Christ! No wonder God will place such heavy stress on acts of service on the day of judgment. He calls upon his church to see the validity of this important spiritual principle: the infinitely great can be seen in the infinitely small; the dramatic can arise from the not so dramatic; life springs from death. Even "a cup of cold water in his name" brings glory. So for the people of God, success must be measured by different standards than those used in the world around us.

A Quiet Prevailing Force

God moves into the fertile, receptive, and open hearts of people. He wins the hearts of people, and he expands his kingdom among the nations of the world. Though we cannot always see the work of God and understand fully his strategy, still we can be confident that he is at work. Nothing can stop the rule of God!

The timing of God often mystifies humans. We usually want to do things quickly, and we sometimes measure success by how quickly a thing can be done. But unwavering patience is essential on the part of the church. The planted seed will bring forth fruit in due season. Despite all the appearances to the contrary, God is at work in our world. The responsibility of God's people is to take his work seriously and to never doubt that his rule will prevail.

There were many doubters in the early days of God's kingdom. For example, when Pliny the Younger (62-113 A.D.) wrote to the Roman emperor, Trajan, he spoke of Rome's efforts to stop Christianity:

> The matter seemed to me to justify my consulting you, especially on account of the number of those in peril; for many persons of all ages and classes and of both sexes are being put in peril by accusation (that they are Christians), and this will go on. The contagion of this superstition has spread not only in the cities, but in the vil-

lages and rural districts as well; yet it seems capable of being checked and set right.[12]

Pliny the Younger overlooked one thing, which is still being overlooked today. The quiet, prevailing rule of God.

---

[1] Alfred Edersheim, *The Life And Times Of Jesus The Messiah*, Vol. 1 (Grand Rapids: William B. Eerdmans Publishing Co., 1953), p. 593.

[2] K.C. Pillai, *Light Through An Eastern Window* (New York: Speller and Sons, 1963), p. 100.

[3] For further background on mustard trees, read E.W.G. Masterman, "Mustard," *The International Standard Bible Encyclopedia*, Vol. 3 (Grand Rapids: William B. Eerdmans Publishing Co., 1957), pp. 2101-2102.

[4] J.D. Douglas, "Leaven," *The New Bible Dictionary* (Grand Rapids: William B. Eerdmans Publishing Co., 1975), p. 725.

[5] For additional background on bread making and leaven, see W.J. Martin, "Bread," *Rediscovering The Parables* (New York: Charles Scribner's Sons, 1966), p. 117; Douglas, ed., op. cit., pp. 165-166.

[6] For additional reading on symbolic significance of "leaven," see H.F. Beck, "Leaven," *The Interpreter's Dictionary of the Bible*, Vol. 3 (Nashville: Abingdon Press, 1962), p. 105.

[7] Edersheim, *The Life And Times Of Jesus The Messiah*, Vol. 1, pp. 586-587.

[8] For additional reading on planting customs and seed time, see J.L. Kelso, "Agriculture," *The New Bible Dictionary*, p. 19; Emmet Russell, "Agriculture," *The Zondervan Pictorial Bible Dictionary* (Grand Rapids: Zondervan Publishing House, 1963), pp. 20-21.

[9] John M'Clintock and James Strong, "Harvest," *Cyclopaedia of Biblical, Theological and Ecclesiastical Literature*, Vol. 4 (New York: Harper and Brothers, 1891), pp. 93-94.

[10] Archibald M. Hunter, *Interpreting the Parables* (Philadelphia: The Westminster Press, 1960), p. 47; Jeremias, *Rediscovering The Parables*, p. 119.

[11] John Bright, *The Kingdom of God* (Nashville: Abingdon Press, 1953), p. 218.

[12] For the entire letter by Pliny the Younger to Trajan, see Henry Bettenson, ed., *Documents of the Christian Church* (New York: Oxford University Press, 1967), pp. 3-4.

Caution— God At Work 4

Bulldozers, earthmovers, open ditches, mounds of dirt, sand, and gravel—whenever you see these you usually see blinking yellow lights and a large sign reading "Caution—Men At Work."

Similarly, what Jesus said and did serves as a "blinking yellow light" to signify "Caution—God At Work!" Jesus drew attention to the work, purpose, and accomplishment of God. He showed how God was and is working out his own purpose.

But why was God at work in Christ? After creation, why didn't God simply withdraw? God could have allowed people to go their own way. Instead, he set about to accomplish something more with his creation. Far from withdrawing, God became deeply and compassionately involved with his lonely, guilty, fearful, and insecure human creatures. It is his nature to want to mend broken people.

We now come to a group of parables that reveal these truths about the nature of God. These parables have two major characteristics. First, each of these parables was addressed to the opponents of Jesus.[1] Jesus addressed the parable of the two sons to the chief priests and elders of the people (Matt. 21:28). He delivered the parable of the two debtors to Simon the Pharisee (Luke 7:40). And he spoke the parable of the workers in the vineyard to several of the scribes and Pharisees (Matt. 20:1). It seems that the main object of the parables is to defend the gospel against critics who fail to see that God cares about sinners and who are particularly offended by Jesus' practice of eating with the despised.[2]

". . . God's punctuation mark for history is in the shape of a cross."

Each of these parables is distinguished by a second characteristic. At the heart of the Christian faith is a strange paradox. If we fail to understand this paradox, we fall into the tragedy of the Pharisees, chief priests, and scribes, having no defense against religious bigotry, prejudice, hatred, legalistic self-righteousness, doctrinal dogmatism, and sectarian institutionalism. Here is the paradox: Love wields more power even when it loses than hate wields when it wins. The greatest power, the best news is the power of self-giving love at the cross of Christ: "But I, when I am lifted up from the earth, will draw all men to myself" (John 12:32).

So God's punctuation mark for history is in the shape of a cross. We celebrate the power of self-giving love when we sing, "In the cross of Christ I glory, towering o'er the wrecks of time." To a world and culture caught up in the achievement of *immediate* results, such a value appears to be sheer insanity. In the deepest understandings of reality, however, we find it true that self-giving love is the greatest power.

Why is self-giving love the greatest power, the best news? Each of the following parables answers this question. Even though it may make no logical sense to human beings, we must remember the sign: "Caution—God At Work!"

Vineyards and Wages

The land and climate of biblical Palestine were almost ideal for vineyards. Rainfall was usually sufficient, and the heat was not too great. Landowners usually planted vineyards on the many hills in Palestine (Isa. 5:1; Jer. 31:5; Amos 9:13). Hired laborers or the landowners themselves usually cultivated the vineyards. But during biblical times it was also a "common practice for a large landowner to rent out his vineyards to a tenant (Song of Sol. 8:11; Matt. 21:33-43)."[3]

The *denarius* was the common silver Roman coin, and it appears to be the daily wage of a laborer, who worked a full Jewish day (from sunrise to sunset). One *denarius* would equal about sixteen cents. The good Samaritan paid two *denarii* to the innkeeper (Luke 10:35), which suggests something of its purchasing power in the time of Christ.[4]

Workers In The Vineyard (*Matt. 20:1-16*)

As Jesus moved into Judea, large crowds followed him, and Pharisees tested him. The legalistic, self-righteous, religious dogmatists among them misunderstood the activity of God and the rule of God in the lives of people. To them the power of self-giving love consisted of an enigma, a puzzle, a vague threat. To them Jesus said, "Let me tell you a story."

A man has a vineyard and goes out early one morning to hire people to work in it. He hires several at sunrise and agrees to pay them a denarius, a daily wage. About nine in the morning, he realizes that he has so much work in the vineyard that he needs more workers. So he goes down to the marketplace, where men are standing around talking about the Romans and the weather, and hires them to work in his vineyard. At noon, he realizes there is still a lot of work to be done in the vineyard, so he goes back to the marketplace to hire additional laborers. And again at three in the afternoon, he hires still more. And, then, do you know what the landowner does? At the very last hour of the workday, with only one more hour of sun left in the day, he hires additional workers to labor in his vineyard.

At the end of the day, it comes time to pay the laborers. As he starts to pay the last ones hired, he realizes that they will take home practically nothing to pay for their daily food, clothing, and housing. So he does a great thing! He pays them a *full* day's wage—a *denarius*. Then, he pays those who had worked all day the same standard wage for a day's labor. But they begin to complain, feeling they have been unjustly treated. The landowner answers each one of them, "Friend, I'm not being unfair to you. Didn't you agree to work for a *denarius*? As for the men who were hired last, I decided to give them the same as I gave you. Don't I have that right? Could it be that you are envious because I am generous?

Jesus turned then to his opponents, who were there among his disciples. "Now do you see," he says in effect, "why God works the way he does?" Self-giving love is God's very nature. The single, most powerful force in the world is the self-giving love of God, as displayed in Jesus. It is, in fact, the only force that overcomes hate, sin, and death. It is his very nature to be loving. It's not that we deserve his love. We are loved by God because of who he is, not because of who we are. God is like a landowner who pays his employees not according to *their* merits but according to *his* nature. We can never fully understand God's grace. God's self-giving love cannot be bound by our laws, nor by our economics. Who are we to say how much love God should show to people?

The Two Sons *(Matt. 21:28-32)*

Why does self-giving love wield such great power? Why is it that God has opened his rule to the totally lost—the prostitutes and tax collectors? This is precisely the question the chief priests and elders focused upon when they asked Jesus, "By what authority are you doing these things?" (Matt. 21:23). Their inquiry provided Jesus the opportunity to tell another story.

71

One day a man who has two sons tells each of them to go to work in the family vineyard. One son refuses at first to go but later changes his mind and goes. The second son immediately answers, "I will," but he does not go.

"Which of these two sons did the father's will?" asked Jesus. The chief priests and elders answered, "The first son did the father's will." Then Jesus said to them, "The tax collectors and the prostitutes are entering the kingdom of God ahead of you. For John the Baptist came to show you the way of righteousness and you did not believe him, but the tax collectors and prostitutes did. And even after you saw this, you did not repent and believe him."

". . . what power has a religion . . . that exalts doctrinal dogmatism and gets nervous about grace . . . ."

The rule of God has been offered to all, Jesus says in effect. Many lost people eventually accept it. But many good, religious people appear to do so but actually are refusing. God's self-giving love wins the hearts and souls of the very people who appear to be far from God. Look how powerful God's self-giving love really is. It changes them from sinners to saints, from persecutors to preachers, from enemies to friends of God. What else can reach sinners who are sick and hurting! What else can offer healing, wholeness, and help! When self-giving love is offered to sinners, it can bring about repentance and change. *Self-giving love is the greatest power and the best news because nothing else has such power to change people.*

So the rule of God is the rule of self-giving love. It meets sinners where they are, and it changes them. In contrast, what power has a religion that draws the self-righteous and bars sinners, that exalts doctrinal dogmatism and gets nervous about grace, that endlessly repeats its traditions and is silent about self-giving love. Its only effect is to build a wall between its members and God. So tax collectors and prostitutes enter the kingdom of God ahead of the leaders of such a religion. To substitute something else in the place of God's self-giving love makes repentance and obedience impossible.

Debt And Debtors

The ancient world practiced severe treatment against debtors, often without regard to their ability or their intention to repay. In Athens, before democratic rights were established, a creditor could demand the slave-labor of his debtor or of members of the debtor's family as surety of payment. Roman law provided punishment by imprisonment to debtors.[5]

The idea of holding a debtor was to force him to sell whatever property he might secretly own, have the debtor's relatives pay his debt, or have the debtor and his family work off the debt.

In spite of legal restrictions, the entire system of debts and sureties was recklessly abused in the ancient world. The prophets frequently condemned violations. Ezekiel and Nehemiah called their contemporaries back to a strict observance of the law, where mercy and justice were intended to prevail (Ezek. 18:8, 13, 17; 22:12; Neh. 5:6-13).[6]

Two Debtors *(Luke 7:36-50)*

Simon the Pharisee invited Jesus to a special dinner, probably in his honor, with other Pharisees. (Since it was considered a meritorious act to invite a synagogue speaker to a meal, some have inferred that Jesus might have just completed a sermon in the local synagogue.)[7] Suddenly, a sinful woman (likely a prostitute) entered the room. Against the custom of the day, she unbound her hair in the presence of the men. Then, she broke the neck of an alabaster jar of perfume and began to anoint Jesus' feet with it. She spread the perfume on Jesus' feet with her hair. It was a shocking scene to Simon and his guests; and it provided them with clear-cut proof that Jesus was not really who he said he was, or he would not have allowed this sinner to approach and touch him.

Why do you suppose he did allow it? Could it be that her self-giving love was a response of gratitude, rather than one of immoral intent? Was there something in her action that Jesus recognized was missing in the formal politeness of the Pharisees? In answer, Jesus told his fellow dinner guests a story.

Two men owed money to a certain moneylender. The first man owed him 500 denarii, and the other owed 50. Neither man had enough money to pay off his debt, so the moneylender canceled the debts of both.

"Which man," Jesus asked, "felt a deeper thankfulness and gratitude?" Simon replied that the one who had the greater debt canceled would feel the deepest gratitude.

Jesus then turned toward the woman and told Simon that her sins had been forgiven—"for she has loved much." In effect, Jesus entreated Simon: "Don't you understand? She's closer to God than you are! She's trying to show her gratitude for the power of self-giving love that God has shown her. But you, Simon, are thankful for very little."

Self-giving love has the power to produce gratitude in the life of a forgiven sinner. Jesus apparently had met this woman before and had assured her of her forgiveness by God. Upon seeing him again, she showed her boundless gratitude in the only way she knew how. Her life had been touched by the power of self-giving love. Simon, on the other hand, felt closer to God because he could point to his piety, civic achievement, and moral superiority. The clear lesson of this event is that those who feel a deep gratitude for their personal forgiveness by God are closer to God and to his rule than many religious persons who trust in their own abilities.

Good News In Strange Circumstances

If hatred, religious prejudice, and bigotry ever looked like winners, they did so on the day of Jesus Christ's death. Here was God's Son, who had never harmed another creature, abused and mocked. He preached and practiced love, only to be crucified and apparently conquered. But that's only the way it appeared. In the plan of God, much more happened that day:

Although he was a son, he learned obedience

75

from what he suffered, and, once made perfect, he became the source of eternal salvation for all who obey him and was designated by God to be high priest, in the order of Melchizedek.

Hebrews 5:8-10

In him we have redemption through his blood, the forgiveness of sins, in accordance with the riches of God's grace that he lavished on us with all wisdom and understanding.

Ephesians 1:7-8

But we preach Christ crucified: a stumbling block to Jews and foolishness to Gentiles, but to those whom God has called, both Jews and Greeks, Christ the power of God and the wisdom of God.

1 Corinthians 1:23-24

God's love for people, as shown in the death of his Son, is the best news ever announced.

Where The Power Is

It is a temptation to feel that the power in Christianity may be found in doctrinal rightness or institutional correctness. We still are tempted to think that we can attract more people if we employ methods other than love. Yet, Jesus said, "But I, when I am lifted up . . . will draw all men to myself" (John 12:32). We can be totally confident that the *power* that is at the heart of the Christian faith is the power of self-giving love and nothing less. The activity of God at work among his people is the power of self-giving love. We are to love those within and those outside the church. We must tell and show people that we love them. So, it is important that we not only agree with the doctrine of love but that we practice love. That's God's way of working.

Winning Through Defeat

What lessons may we learn from God's activity on the cross of Jesus? There are two lessons: (1) hate never looks more like a loser than when it wins; (2) love never looks more like a winner than when defeated. Let's consider each of these.

Hate never looks more like a loser than when it wins. In any given moment, a nail, a scourge, a bitter cup, or a hammer's blow may appear to win. A good life breathes its last breath. Hatred's way of getting back at people is almost unbelievable. It can, in the name of "right," produce the greatest "wrongs." No matter what it looks like it is doing, hate can only destroy; it has no power to build. Hate can seduce, but it cannot convince. Hate can only manipulate; it has no power to create trust and commitment.

"Love never looks more like a winner than when it is defeated."

Love never looks more like a winner than when it is defeated. Love has the power to endure. Reviled, love does not return the same. Hurt, it does not return hurt. Bruised and defeated on a cross, love proves victorious. For beyond the moment of death on a cross, it endures as self-giving love—the greatest power ever known on earth. Ernest Freemont Tittle puts it in eloquent language:

You may place upon the brow of truth a crown of thorns. You may mock truth, scourge it, spit upon it. You may even crucify it between two lies. But ever on the third day it rises from the dead, begins to be seen, heard, and heeded. In any given twenty-four hours love may prove to be no match at all for sheer brute force. A crossbeam, some nails, a hammer, a spear, a sponge dipped in vinegar and lifted to lips in anguish; a loud inarticulate cry as one who has put his trust in love gives up the ghost. But when sheer brute force has had its little day of triumph and vanished from the earth—love is more than ever alive and begins to govern the ages.[8]

---

[1] Joachim Jeremias, *Rediscovering the Parables* (New York: Charles Scribner's Sons, 1966), p. 98.

[2] Loc. cit.

[3] For background information on vineyards, see J.F. Ross, "Vine, Vineyard," *The Interpreter's Dictionary of the Bible*, Vol. 4 (Nashville: Abingdon Press, 1962), pp. 785-786; Steven Barabas, "Vine, Vineyard," *The Zondervan Pictorial Bible Dictionary* (Grand Rapids: Zondervan Publishing House, 1963), pp. 881-882.

[4] D.H. Wheaton, "Money," *The New Bible Dictionary* (Grand Rapids: William B. Eerdmans Publishing Co., 1975), pp. 840-841; Alfred Edersheim, *The Life and Times of Jesus the Messiah*, Vol. 2 (Grand Rapids: William B. Eerdmans Publishing Co., 1953), p. 417.

[5] C. Kathleen Freeman, *The Murder of Herodes and Other Trials From The Athenian Law Courts* (New York: W. W. Norton and Co., Inc., 1946), pp. 14-30.

[6] G.A. Banois, "Debt, Debtor," *The Interpreter's Dictionary of the Bible*, Vol. 1, p. 810; A.E. Willingale, "Debt, Debtor," *The New Bible Dictionary*, p. 304.

[7] Jeremias, op. cit., p. 99.

[8] Ernest Freemont Tittle, *Jesus After Nineteen Centuries* (New York: The Abingdon Press, 1932), pp. 142-143.

How To Live And Like It 5

The primary concern of the kingdom of God is people. Since the kingdom of God is composed of people, the invitation to be in the kingdom's domain is marked by a personal response to a personal invitation: "Come to me, all *you* who are weary and burdened, and I will give *you* rest. Take my yoke upon *you* and learn from me, for I am gentle and humble in heart, and *you* will find rest for *your* souls. For my yoke is easy and my burden is light" (Matt. 11:28-30).

What, then, is a person's response to the rule of God for his life? How is life in the kingdom to be lived? What should we expect to see in the life of a person committed to the divine rule?

Our best picture of life in the kingdom comes from the parables of Jesus. His parables portray for us the life of discipleship. To catch his meaning, we must understand the symbols Jesus used.

Hidden Treasure And Pearls

Ancient story telling frequently focused on stories of hidden treasure and precious stones. Even today, the Middle East gives up its secrets of hidden treasure. Recall, for example, the discovery of the Qumran Scrolls along the Dead Sea. More recently archaeologists uncovered the king of Macedonia's tomb in Greece. Even peasants will occasionally discover coins, precious stones, and other artifacts of great value.

In the ancient world, people buried treasure for two reasons: (1) It was the safest way to keep personal wealth (safer than carrying it on one's person or keeping it at home, where security was primitive at best).[2] (2) Since Palestine was frequently invaded (usually being the plunder of private citizens), treasure often was buried at a time of serious threat.[3]

One particular treasure of great value in the ancient world was the pearl. In search of the extraordinary, pearl merchants traveled as far as India, the Red Sea, and the Persian Gulf. A person might have sold everything he or she owned to purchase a single pearl. The value of pearls was not only commercial, for pearls were seen as symbols of eternal beauty (Rev. 21:21).

Treasure In Field, Pearl of Value (Matt. 13:44-46)

Jesus showed how a person would respond to the rule of God by telling this story:

A treasure box filled with precious jewels and coins had lain buried in a field for many years. While plowing the field one day, a man struck the

treasure box with the blade of his plow. He dug in and around the box until he unearthed it. He opened the treasure box, seeing before him precious coins and unique and valuable stones of greater wealth than he had ever dreamed. Immediately, he hid the treasure in the field in a place known only to him. Then do you know what the man did? In the joy of his discovery, he sold everything he had, went to the owner, and bought that field.

By this parable, Jesus in effect has said, "That's the way a person responds to the rule of God for his life." God offers salvation, a relationship, guidance, forgiveness, security, identity, an understanding of death, and hope for the future. When a person discovers this "treasure," he comes to God with great joy.

What about the ethics of purchasing a field while not revealing the discovery of the treasure to the owner? The thrust of his parable points toward the *value* of the treasure. The finder does not steal the treasure, but first legally buys the field.[4] The joy of discovery and the willingness to give up everything is the point Jesus makes.

A similar parable points to yet another dimension of our response:

A pearl merchant traveled far and wide in search of the finest pearls. In his search one day, he discovered a pearl without equal, a pearl beyond any value he had ever known. Immediately and without hesitation, he sold all of his other pearls of lesser value and everything he owned. With urgency, he bought the single pearl of greatest value.

So Jesus has said, in effect, "This too, is the way a person responds to the rule of God for his own life." It is a matter of *radical urgency*. That valuable discovery for his life eliminates any possibility of procrastination. He finds in the rule of God more than he had thought he would ever possess. He wants to respond to God immediately!

Talents And Denarii

In Greek currency, a *denarius* is worth about seventeen cents and a *talent* is equal to about one thousand twenty dollars. For a man to owe a king ten thousand *talents* means that he owes him $10,200,000—an incredible debt.[5]

To grasp the unbelievable amount of such a debt, let's calculate how long it would take to repay such a huge sum in the ancient world. In earning seventeen cents a day, which was the standard daily wage of a laborer in the time of Jesus, it would take 1,644 years to pay off a debt of $10,200,000. And that calculation does not include any interest on the principal. If the principal carried eight percent interest, the man, who began working in the time of Jesus, would have been able to pay off his debt in the year of the American Revolution—1776! Obviously, the man would have owed a debt too great for repayment!

On the other hand, a debt of 100 *denarii* would have been about seventeen dollars, a debt capable of repayment.

The Unmerciful Servant *(Matt. 18:21-35)*

One parable was occasioned when Peter asked Jesus, "Lord, how many times shall I forgive my brother when he sins against me? Up to seven times?" "Seven" symbolized to Peter infinity, perfection, or completion. Jesus answered, "I tell you, not seven times, but seventy times seven." "Seventy" symbolized the work of God — infinity times infinity, perfection times perfection, or completion times completion.[6]

Jesus stressed that mercy and forgiveness are at the heart of discipleship when he told this parable:

A king settled his accounts with his servants and confronted one debtor with a debt of ten thousand talents. Since the man was not able to pay such an incredible debt, the master ordered that he, his family, and all he had be sold into slavery in order to pay off the debt. But the servant fell to his knees and pleaded with the king, "Be patient with me, and I will pay you back everything." So the king took pity on him and canceled the debt, letting his servant go free. But the servant went out and found one of his fellow servants who owed him a hundred denarii. He grabbed him by the neck and demanded, "Pay back everything you owe me in full!" His fellow servant fell to his knees and pleaded with him, "Be patient with me, and I will pay you back." But the servant refused and had his fellow servant thrown in prison until he could pay the debt. When the other servants saw what had happened, they immediately told the king everything. The king called the servant in and told him, "I canceled all your debt because you begged me to do so. I had mercy upon you. Why didn't you show mercy upon your fellow servant?" The king then turned him over to the jailors and ordered him to pay back what he owed.

So the answer Jesus gave to Peter was: "See how the rule of God in your life calls for mercy?" The rule of God in your life cancels your debt to God, offering you full, perfect, and complete forgiveness. Your response to the rule of God calls for mercy toward others.

Rock And Sand

For security in the ancient world, people depended greatly upon the foundations of buildings and city walls. The ancients built buildings that endured upon solid rock.[7] Indeed, Solomon built his magnificent temple to God upon a solid rock foundation (1 Kings 5:17).

Only a person wishing to build a temporary structure would erect it upon sand. In ancient Palestine, autumn rains and winds lashed at every building. Without a firm foundation, a building would be destroyed in a matter of moments!

The Two Builders *(Matt. 7:24-29)*

Jesus spoke this parable to the great mass of people who gathered to hear his sermon on the mount. His sermon focused on a new life, the rule of God in one's life. It would be a life that begins with self-denial, that builds on faith, not anxiety, whose ethic is controlled by God, and that relies upon the promises of Jesus. These are words filled with hope and provide an option to an old way of doing things.

The climax of the Sermon on the Mount presented another parable:

A man of prudence and judgment decided to build his house upon a solid foundation of rock.

It cost him much time and expense to build it. He thought not only of the moment but of the future. So when the autumn rains came and the winds blew against his house, it stood strong and firm because it had been built upon solid rock. But another man, a man not so prudent and wise, built his house thinking only of the moment, not of the future. He built his house upon a foundation of sand. And when the fall rains and winds beat against his house, it collapsed because it had no foundation.

The message of this parable concerned a person's response to the rule of God. "If you obey me," Jesus said in effect, "you will weather the storm. Neglect my words and you court disaster." The wise man is one who builds on the sure foundation of total commitment to Christ. The foolish man is the one who builds on the weak foundation of hesitation and timidity.

Joy-Filled Living

Discipleship in the kingdom of God calls for joyful commitment. Response to God's rule for one's life has two prongs: (1) what you give up, and (2) what you get. With the offer of God's rule comes a demand: "Sell all." There is a radical urgency to give up everything that might come between one's discipleship and God:

> . . . If anyone would come after me, he must deny himself and take up his cross daily and follow me. For whoever wants to save his life will lose it, but whoever loses his life for me will save it.
>
> Luke 9:23-24

Society calls this approach to life "foolish." The culture says, "Look out for self!" Jesus says, "Die to self." Jesus calls for complete surrender to one's past and, if necessary, to one's family:

> . . . If anyone comes to me and does not hate (love less) his father and mother, his wife and children, his brothers and sisters—yes, even his own life—he cannot be my disciple. And anyone who does not carry his cross and follow me cannot be my disciple.
>
> Luke 14:25-27

Matthew left his tax collecting. Peter, Andrew, James, and John left their fishing nets. Saul of Tarsus left his promising law career. Why? Because each had found "a treasure," "a pearl." With self-denial, concern for others, and a life of service, each finds his "life." With radical urgency, each "sells all" to follow Jesus.

"Joyful commitment not only entails what one gives up, but what one receives."

Joyful commitment not only entails what one gives up, but what one receives. To a life burdened with guilt, broken with loneliness, shot through with insecurity and filled with aimless wandering, God offers his rule that meets every personal need. What he gives to our lives is greater than anything we could desire or wish. Joy rules the heart and becomes the badge of the Christian life: "Rejoice in the Lord always. I will say it again: Rejoice!" (Phil. 4:4). There is always great joy in the

Christian community when they have given themselves in total commitment to Christ. Lack of joy marks self-centered people, even religious people.

A Call For Mercy

Discipleship in the kingdom of God calls for mercy. The call to follow Jesus includes demonstrating to our fellowman the same mercy we have received from God. There is no limit to the mercy of God. We were burdened by a debt impossible to repay, but he has *canceled* our debt. Compassion and grace spring from the deep heart of God. His eternal purpose of forming a people in Christ (Eph. 1:3-14; 1 Pet. 2:9-10) led him to show mercy and pardon to bring us into his family. The human offense of sin against God is so incredibly great that divine mercy is the only hope for carrying through God's will for mankind.

Having received mercy from God, believers channel mercy to others. Mercy does not paste labels on people, harden the categories, or manipulate people. Mercy listens; grace forgives. Secular people have no desire to be in a church that treats them like they are treated every day in the world. But a church whose members forgive one another and foster a loving spirit will attract the seekers. In secular life, mercy and grace are the scarcest products of all.

A Call For Action

Discipleship calls for action—obedience to Jesus. Jesus presses the "now-relationship" with him. Sad is the life that hears the words of Jesus and plans "someday" to come to him. Disaster and tragedy mark the lives of many people who pay lip service to Jesus but whose lives cannot bear up under the slightest wind.

Urgent action in immediate obedience to Christ's words springs from the ultimate test of every life. There's no question about it: the rains *will* fall; the winds *will* blow; the streams *will* rise. Every person's life is tested by crises, and the storms hit hard: cancer, unemployment, moving, death. There is a difference between the disciple's life and the nondisciple's life but it is not in the lack of crises. The difference is in the foundation. Obedient action, Jesus says, is the foundation that will bear up under stress. Lip service, however, invests nothing for a rainy day.

---

[1] Nolan B. Harmon, ed. *The Interpreter's Bible*, Vol. IV (Nashville: Abingdon Press, 1951), p. 694.

[2] Nolan B. Harmon, ed. *The Interpreter's Bible*, Vol. 7 (Nashville: Abingdon Press, 1951), p. 419; Note: Joachin Jeremias, *Rediscovering The Parables* (New York: Charles Scribner's Sons, 1966), p. 156.

[3] Alfred Edersheim, *The Life and Times of Jesus The Messiah*, Vol. I (Grand Rapids: Wm. B. Eerdmans Publishing Co., 1953), pp. 595-596.

[4] J.D. Douglas, ed. *The New Bible Dictionary* (Grand Rapids: Wm. B. Eerdmans Publishing Co., 1975), pp. 840-841.

[5] Merrill C. Tenney, ed. *The Zondervan Pictorial Bible Dictionary* (Grand Rapids: Zondervan Publishing House, 1963), p. 590; Douglas, op. cit., p. 898.

[6] Douglas, op. cit., p. 439.

It's Later Than You Think 6

I once read a story about Satan meeting with his evil spirits to plan his strategy against human beings. "Who will go to earth and persuade people to lose their souls?" he asked. The first evil spirit said, "I will go and tell them there is no heaven." A second evil spirit said, "I will go, and I will tell them there is no hell." Then, a third spirit responded, "I will go, and I will tell them there is no hurry." Satan told the third spirit, "Go immediately."

Jesus, on the other hand, has taught us the urgency of accepting and following the kingdom. It has come; it is at hand; it is here. Jesus pressed the *urgency* of obedience. With history rapidly moving toward a final moment of judgment, there is no time to lose! Seeing the sweep of God's grand design and purpose, Jesus insisted that it is the last hour!

But encourage one another daily, as long as it is called Today, so that none of you may be hardened by sin's deceitfulness.

Hebrews 3:13

I tell you, now is the time of God's favor, now is the day of salvation.

2 Corinthians 6:2b

How late is it? Why is there urgency for accepting God's rule? Jesus has answered these questions by way of his parables that serve to say, "It's later than you think!"

Virgins

Several of the ancient Mediterranean people considered virgins of tremendous value to their culture, customs, and ceremonies. The vestal virgins of Rome, for instance, received special privileges for rendering service in special religious ceremonies. The story of Esther indicates that people looked upon a virgin as a candidate for royalty. Apparently, her freedom from sexual relationships allowed her complete devotion and total commitment necessary for leadership.[1]

Young virgins traditionally served in several ceremonies, including marriage. Ancient customs spell out their place in the marriage ceremony. They would stay in a special room at a traveler's inn located near the gates of the city. There they would wait for the bridegroom and his bridal party to arrive for the wedding. The bridesmaids carried special torches (not household lamps), which were

soaked in oil and handed down from one generation of family weddings to the next. Custom also
said that the bridegroom and his party must arrive
precisely at midnight. Usually his arrival was announced by a member of his party blowing a
trumpet or calling out from the walls of the city.
The bridemaids then lit their torches and accompanied the bridegroom to the home of the bride. The
wedding celebration came to a conclusion when
the bridegroom went to the home of the bride and
she accompanied him to his parents' house.[2] Some
of these customs still continue in Palestine today.

Since a torch would burn only a few minutes,
thoughtful preparation included taking plenty of
oil in a small jar. A bridegroom might be delayed
because of necessary bargaining between his parents and hers concerning the gifts to be paid to the
bride's parents. After the arrival of the bridegroom,
a special wedding banquet would take place; and
all of those present and prepared for the wedding
feast would be invited to attend. Those who pro-
crastinated and arrived late for the wedding feast
would be refused entry.

The Ten Virgins (Matt. 25:1-13)

In order to stress the *urgency*, the actual *emergency*, of the coming of the kingdom of God to a
person's life, Jesus related a parable.

**The kingdom of heaven will be like ten virgins
who were going to meet the bridegroom. Five of
the bridesmaids took enough oil for their torches
and no more. But the other five bridesmaids took
enough oil for their torches and some in reserve.
Not knowing exactly when the bridegroom and**

his party would come, the ten bridesmaids waited. The evening wore on into the late hours. Since the bridegroom's bargaining took longer than expected, the bridesmaids became very drowsy and fell asleep. At midnight, they were awakened with the announcement: "Here's the bridegroom! Come out to meet him!" Then all the bridesmaids woke up and lit their torches. But five of the torches would no longer burn for there was not enough oil. So the five bridesmaids who owned these torches said to the others, "Give us some of your oil for our torches will not burn." "No," said the five wise virgins, "There won't be enough for all of us. You'll have to go to those who sell oil and buy from them." So the five bridesmaids went off searching for oil for their torches. While they were gone, the bridegroom arrived. The five virgins who were ready went in with him to the wedding banquet, after which the doors were closed. The celebration began, with eating, drinking, music, and dancing. Later, the other five bridesmaids arrived pleading, "Open the door for us!" But the bridegroom replied, "I don't know you." And the door remained shut.

After Jesus finished, we can imagine him leaning forward, looking into the eyes of those around him as he said, "Therefore keep watch, because you do not know the day or the hour." To those on the outer edge of commitment to him, Jesus would stress, "See how critical it is for you to accept now the rule of God in your own lives." Jesus would continue to press the point: "The wedding day is here! The bridegroom will arrive at any moment! Get ready for the wedding banquet! If you accept

God's rule, you may attend the wedding banquet! And then the door will be shut!" Jesus urges, "It's later than you think."

A Fig Tree

The ancient world appreciated the fig tree so much that some people considered it almost sacred. It symbolized prosperity, and its shade symbolized God's great favor. "In Hellenistic times figs were considered so important to the national economy that the Greeks made special laws to regulate their export."[3]

The fruit of the fig appears before the leaves. Therefore, the ancient Jewish law prohibited eating any fruit during the first three years of a tree's growth:

> When you enter the land and plant any kind of fruit tree, regard its fruit as forbidden. For three years you are to consider it forbidden; it must not be eaten. In the fourth year all its fruit will be holy, an offering of praise to the Lord. But in the fifth year you may eat its fruit. In this way your harvest will be increased. I am the Lord your God.
>
> Leviticus 19:23-25

Based on this law, the "barren fig tree" of the parable would likely be at least six years old, since its first three years are bypassed. A "barren fig tree" would suggest lack of prosperity and lack of God's favor. Prized for its delicious and bountiful fruit, a fig tree that does not produce would be of no value and would be cut down.[4]

The Barren Fig Tree *(Luke 13:6-9)*

Here is another story Jesus told to illustrate the

urgency of accepting the rule of God in one's life:

A man who planted a vineyard included in it (as often was the case) a fig tree. Now, the owner didn't look for fruit from the fig tree for the first three years. But at the end of the first three years, he expected it to produce. So while in his vineyard one day, he looked at the fig tree. There was not one fig on the tree! So the owner waited a year and again looked for fruit from the fig tree. No figs appeared. He waited yet another year and still no sign of the fig tree bearing fruit. The owner realized that the fig tree was using valuable nourishment that could be used for the grapes. (After all, he could have planted grapes in place of the fig tree.) So he ordered his gardener to cut it down but the gardener replied, "Sir, let me do something we normally do not do to fig trees—let me dig around this one. Maybe it's not getting enough air, water, or nourishment. I'll dig deep and pull the earth back up on it. Let me do something else unusual—let me fertilize it." The owner gave him permission but added, "if after one more year of you doing everything you can and it still does not produce, cut it down."

After Jesus had thus caught the attention of those listening to him, he would say in effect, "That's how urgent it is to accept the rule of God in your own life!"

God keeps coming to us, giving us every opportunity, and never giving up on us. He gets our attention and is willing to wait patiently for us. He does the unusual, taking extraordinary action in order that our lives might bear fruit. But if after every opportunity we do not accept the rule of God, we will not have another chance.

Now, But Not Forever

Using simple symbols familiar to his audience, Jesus taught a profound truth concerning the nature of the kingdom of God. That truth is that God's mercy is extended *now, but not forever!* At the very heart and center of everything we know about God is his *mercy, grace,* and *loving kindness*. He allows us every opportunity to come to the wedding banquet and to bear fruit. As to whether or not his mercy is a part of our lives is not his choice but ours. He gives us every opportunity to be part of his possessions, to be in his family, and to be a part of his body.

But Jesus in essence says, "It's later than you think!" The time is now; the bridegroom is coming; the owner is looking for a fruitful tree. It is urgent for every person to accept God's mercy *today,* for God's mercy is extended now, but not forever.

"The truth is that God's mercy is extended now, but not forever!"

I have had the opportunity of knowing people who had accepted God's mercy and did not know that a tragedy was about to strike their lives. They were, however, wise people who acted when they had the opportunity, who prepared in the here and now. They did not know it at the time, but there was little time left. Then, I think of other people who have had numerous opportunities to accept

God's mercy. They had no way of knowing that tragedy was on its way. They did not have much time, but they foolishly presumed there would be *more* time. There wasn't! Jesus says, "It's later than you think!"

Christianity stresses the importance of the *here and now*. Contrary to popular notions, Christianity does not lay its greatest emphasis upon the future. God's mercy is extended *now*, and the opportunity for a productive life is now. Our lives move closer and closer to judgment. God's mercy ought not to be misunderstood as weakness. Today is what we have, so a wise person acts now. "It's later than you think!"

Beyond Our Control

For sheer drama, the scene of Paul speaking to Felix and his wife Drusilla is hard to match. Paul spoke to them about faith in Christ Jesus. As he stressed "righteousness, self-control, and the judgment to come, Felix was afraid and said, 'That's enough for now! You may leave. *When I find it convenient,* I will send for you' " (Acts 24:25). As far as we know, Felix never became a Christian. It was never convenient!

To the person who believes he has time within his control, Jesus says, "It's later than you think!" How tempting it is to think that life itself is under control since we've been able to control so much of our lives. We've conquered many diseases and space, communicated across the earth, and built large arsenals of nuclear weapons—all of which may lead to a false sense of security. But we cannot control time; it's beyond our control.

Only God controls time. "No one knows about that day or hour, not even the angels in heaven, nor the Son, but only the Father" (Matt. 24:36). Jesus stresses over and over the urgency of accepting the rule of God today: "Therefore keep watch, because you do not know on what day your Lord will come . . . So you also must be ready, because the Son of Man will come at an hour when you do not expect him" (Matt 24:42, 44). "It's later than you think!"

I'll Do It Tomorrow

Why do we procrastinate? Why do we delay? Why do we depend upon "tommorrow"?

Perhaps a part of the answer can be found in the nature of our lives. Most of our lives are spent in endeavors that allow a *second chance*. Ours is the society that invented erasers and correction fluid. We usually get a second chance, another opportunity to correct, improve, or try again.

". . . in Greek mythology, 'opportunity' is pictured as a beautiful maiden who passed by a person's life only once."

Frankly, it's very tempting to think that we will always get a second chance. But when it comes to Gods' reign in our lives, we are advised to not put confidence in "tomorrow," not to plan on further opportunities:

> Now listen, you who say, "Today or tomorrow we will go to this or that city, spend a year there, carry on business and make money." Why, you do

not even know what will happen tomorrow. What is your life? You are a mist that appears for a little while and then vanishes. Instead, you ought to say, "If it is the Lord's will, we will live and do this or that."

James 4:13-15

Jesus never says, "There's plenty of time!" He calls us to *act;* he places no premium on caution. Satan says, "No hurry. Do it tomorrow!" Jesus knows that when the last day of repentance passes, it is *too* late. One who lets God rule his life seizes the opportunity.

In Greek mythology, "opportunity" is pictured as a beautiful maiden who passes by a person's life only once. The Greeks picture her having long hair, flowing down the front of her face and body. As she passes by, one must seize "opportunity," for she has no hair flowing down her back. There will not be a second chance.

Realizing the folly of "waiting until tomorrow," Jesus possesses an unequivocal spirit about obeying God. There is no middle ground, no "tomorrow," nor time to count as "ours." There's no time to lose, for time belongs to God. Thus, Jesus worked to the point of exhaustion day and night to bring people to God's rule. John Bright stresses the urgency of Jesus in his fine book, *The Kingdom of God*:

Christ, then, has come to call men to his Kingdom. His mission was not to instruct men in a better and more spiritual ethic, to impart to men a clearer understanding of the character of God, to attack those abuses which had made the Jewish law the stultification of the religious spirit and to suggest certain emendations to that law—in short, to point men the way to be better men. All this he did, indeed, and with a vengeance. But he did it in the dazzling light of the coming Kingdom. His was a call of tremendous urgency, a call of radical decision for that Kingdom? The Kingdom is *right there*, "at hand." It stands at the door and knocks (Luke 12:36, cf. Rev. 3:20). Who will open and let it in? Who will say *Yes* to its coming?[5]

"It's later than you think!"

---

[1] George A. Buttrick, ed., *The Interpreter's Dictionary of the Bible*, Vol. 4 (Nashville: Abingdon Press, 1962), pp. 787-788.

[2] Joachim Jeremias, *Rediscovering the Parables* (New York: Charles Scribner's Sons, 1966), p. 137. For additional background reading on marriage customs surrounding this parable see K.C. Pillai, *Light Through An Eastern Window* (New York: Steller and Sons, 1963), pp. 9-14.

[3] J.D. Douglas, ed., *The New Bible Dictionary* (Grand Rapids: William B. Eerdmans Publishing Co., 1975), p. 422.

[4] For further reading on fig trees, see Alfred Edersheim, *The Life and Times of Jesus the Messiah*, Vol. 2 (Grand Rapids: William B. Eerdmans Publishing Co., 1953), pp. 246-248; Jeremias, *Rediscovering the Parables*, pp. 135-136.

[5] John Bright, *The Kingdom of God* (Nashville: Abingdon Press, 1953), p. 219.

A Call To Action 7

July 4, 1948 is a date that stands out in my memory.

My family had just enjoyed eating a fresh watermelon, and my aunt and uncle had just left for their home. After watering the flower bed on the side of our house, I remember running to the backyard. Suddenly, I fell! The milk bottle, which I had used to water the flowers, had broken and a large piece of glass had cut almost through my left hand. Immediately, my parents took me to Vanderbilt University Hospital, where a surgeon in the emergency room cleaned my hand and prepared it for surgery. I still remember him asking me to make a fist with my left hand. I tried as hard as I could, but none of my fingers would move. My hand failed to respond. It was as though a paralysis gripped it. Only after successful surgery could I make a fist.

This is the way life is at times. The very things you want to do, you don't do. And the very things you don't want to do, you do. We want our lives to improve, but somehow there's a failure to act, a failure to respond to what will improve our lives. We can become gripped with a kind of spiritual and emotional paralysis. Deep feelings of guilt, fear, depression, and loneliness may cause us to feel that circumstances control us. Psychiatrist Martin E.P. Seligman describes depression, which is now at epidemic proportions, as "a belief in one's own *helplessness*." He found in his research that the cloud of depression begins to lift when a person believes that he is not bound by unchangeable circumstances but can take meaningful actions that prove that he is not helpless.[1]

Jesus dealt with similar situations of spiritual and emotional paralysis in people. To them he offered an invitation: "Follow me." Today, Jesus offers depressed people a new option. He calls for us to get up, to act, to respond, to open our hearts to him, and to allow him to free us from the circumstances that cause us to feel helpless.

Why does God call for action? Why doesn't God allow us to be exclusively a meditative or reflective people? Why does God demand something more than an intellectual kind of faith? Why does he use so many injunctions, so many imperatives in Christianity that call for action? The answers to these questions are revealed in the simple, yet powerful, stories of Jesus—his parables.

Public storehouses were well known in the ancient world. Egypt stored government supplies at the cities of Pithom and Raamses. While in Egypt,

Joseph laid up a tremendous supply of corn to be used in the years of drought. In ancient Israel, David, Solomon, Jehoshaphat, and Hezekiah built public storehouses. Such storehouses were quite common in the Mediterranean world.

> The form of one of those ancient granaries is exhibited in a painting of the tomb of Rotei at Beni-Hassan. It consists of a double range of structures resembling ovens built of brick, with an opening at the top of these receptacles, into which the grain measured and noted, is poured til they are full. The mode of emptying them was to open the shutter in the side.[2]

In addition to these public storehouses, large, private storehouses were also known in the ancient world. They housed seed, corn, or grain. Private barns were not places where corn could be kept until it was threshed but were warehouses or stores in which the grain could later be laid up.[3]

Whether a public storehouse or a private barn, a full storehouse was a sign of prosperity (Deut. 28:8; Prov. 3:10; Luke 2:18) and an empty barn indicated hard times (Joel 1:17).[4]

The Rich Fool (Luke 12:16-21)

On one occasion, Jesus was called upon to resolve a family feud. Two brothers were concerned about who would get the most inheritance, property, and money. From Jesus point of view, to immerse one's self in money-making and to secure one's life with possessions is to miss the point of living! Jesus illustrated the real point with this story:

I want to tell you about the time a man planted a crop, and the ground produced a tremendous harvest. He began to think to himself, "I've never had such a great harvest. I've had good years before when the rain came just at the right time and when the soil produced bountifully. And I've even had crops that produced a hundred times what I planted. But I have never seen a crop like this one! In fact, I have filled up my warehouse to capacity, and I still have so much left. I'm going to have to think about what to do."

So he thought about it, and he said to himself, "I really don't have many warehouses, and I am going to need a place to put this surplus." He told himself, "I have so much left over that I'll never have to worry again. I've got it made. All I'll need to do now is just sit back and enjoy life. I am secure and have everything I need."

Nevertheless, Jesus warned, "God will come to this man and he will say to this man, 'You are living your life as though I do not exist. You're relating to all the events of this harvest and all of your life as though I were not around. You're making your plans, deciding on the future, and making all of your decisions totally without depending on me. You know how foolish this is? Tonight, before you get to use any of these things, build the next warehouse, or relax and enjoy all the things that have come to you, I will require of you your life."

After finishing the story, Jesus may have turned to those in the crowd and in essence said, "This is how it will be with anyone who stores things up for himself but does not rely upon God." A person who lives his life securing it with things has missed the very point of living. God calls for action because he is primary to life. One reason Jesus has called men and women to respond to the kingdom is that God is the only reality that can fill the blankness of our lives. There's nothing more significant than relating to God. A wise person never sees God as negligible or optional. He places God in the hard core of his own life, never in the margins.

"God calls for action because he is primary to life."

The ancients placed tremendous confidence in their "steward." A steward was "an official who controlled the affairs of a large household, overseeing the service at the master's table, directing the household servants, and controlling the household expenses on behalf of the master."[5] The Old Testament frequently refers to stewards or estate managers (Gen. 43:19; 44:4; 1 Kings 16:9; Isa. 22:15).

In New Testament times, stewards were not necessarily slaves but sometimes men of esteem. On occasion, a steward would be selected as the treasurer of a city. Paul described Christian leaders as God's stewards in his church (Titus 1:7).[6]

The Unjust Steward *(Luke 16:1-8)*

The relation between a steward and his master

became the means by which Jesus could teach his followers something important about both the nature of God and the nature of life with God. So the steward became the subject of another parable.

There once was a man who owned a large estate. He had hired a steward to manage it in his absence. On one occasion the owner checked with his manager to see how well the estate was producing. After talking with the steward, the owner began to wonder about him. He wondered if the steward was a careful man or whether, in fact, he was being too wasteful. Was he embezzling the estate? The more the owner of the estate talked with the steward, the more displeased the owner became. He made up his mind to dismiss the steward.

But before such happened, the steward began thinking, "I am going to lose my job. Yet, I'm not strong enough to do harder work; and I've got too much pride to go out and beg." So the steward started thinking about everybody who owed money to the owner of the estate. He went to one debtor and asked, "How much do you owe my master?" And the man said, "Well, I owed him 800 gallons of olive oil." In those days that was a very heavy debt. The steward replied, " I want you to take the bill and write that you owe 400 gallons instead." Next, he went to another man who was indebted to the owner. "What do you owe?", he asked. "I owe him 1,000 bushels of wheat," replied the second man. The steward told him, "I want you to erase the 1,000 and in its place write 800." Then the steward went back to the owner of the estate and told the owner about these men who owed him some money. But he assured the owner, "I'm on top of this thing. I've got it put together, and they're going to pay you. You're not going to lose it all." And do you know what the owner of the estate said to the manager? He said, "You have done a good job!"

Jesus told his disciples, "The master commended the dishonest manager because he acted shrewdly. For the people of this world are more shrewd in dealing with their own kind than are the people of the light" (Luke 16:8). So Jesus commended the steward's action to us because we, like the steward, find ourselves in crises that threaten our very existence. Prudent, responsible action is called for by Christ because of the challenges and pressures which life brings us. We must act and act shrewdly.

Jesus did not commend the dishonesty of this manager, but commended his resolute action. The man didn't become paralyzed and gripped by his crisis. The kingdom of God is composed of people who must take resolute, bold, and shrewd actions.

Wedding Garments

In the ancient world when a wedding was about to take place in a royal palace, the preparations would always be impressive and extensive. A wedding banquet held at the king's palace would mean a large guest list. With the invitation came a special wedding robe, designed especially for the royal occasion, as a present from the king. A robe with the royal seal would be sent to the home of the guest a day or two in advance of the wedding. Each guest, then, would be assured of being properly attired.[7] It would be totally insensitive and unimaginable for a guest to wear his own clothes in place of the one sent by the king. To wear no wedding robe at all would be a serious breach of custom.

But how would a guest come into a banquet room without wearing any kind of wedding garment? Here is one explanation that helps one understand the process of entering a royal wedding banquet:

> When the guests arrive for the wedding, they come first to a sort of porch where there is a tub of water and a servant is in attendance so the guest may wash their feet after having walked in the dusty pathways . . . He holds a very humble and lowly position in the household which he serves . . . This lowly servant would have no authority in the household to challenge a guest who might come without a robe. After washing the feet, the guests pass into a room of the house in which another servant awaits. The task of this servant is to sprinkle rose water on the head and body of the guest. He, like the first servant, has no authority to challenge a guest which might not be properly attired.[8]

If a guest had willfully refused to wear the royal garment, he might properly be dismissed from the wedding banquet.

Guest Without Garment (*Matt. 22:1-14*)

When the chief priests and Pharisees heard the parables of Jesus, they looked for an opportunity to arrest him. Jesus knew that they were gripped in a spiritual paralysis—they had failed to receive the kingdom of God. So he related a parable that showed what was so tragically missing in their lives.

Once there was a king who prepared a formal wedding banquet for his son. As the host, the king sent out all the invitations, prepared the menu, readied the banquet hall, and invited people to come. Then, the king sent out his servants to tell the people, "We're going to have a great banquet. My son is getting married. Everything is ready so come to the wedding banquet." But they paid no attention to this invitation. Some of those who were invited abused and even murdered the king's servants. When the king heard of this he was shocked and enraged. He sent his army out, destroyed the murderers, and burned their city. And then he said to his servants, "The banquet is ready. You are to go out and urgently appeal to people to come to my son's wedding feast. Go out on the street corners and walk down the streets. Whenever you see people, invite them to my son's wedding feast." Soon the wedding banquet hall was filled with all kinds of people: men and women, the young and old, the rich and poor, the various ethnic groups. When the king entered, he looked around to see who had accepted his invitation. But he stared in shock when he saw a man seated at the end of one of the banquet tables without one of the royal wedding robes, which are given to the guest. Thus, the king ordered him to be thrown out of the banquet hall.

Jesus turned to the chief priests and Pharisees and said, "For many are invited, but few are chosen." God offers to people his royal wedding garments of salvation, forgiveness, and relationship. When people try to come into his presence dressed in their own righteousness instead of God's free gift of grace, the result is banishment from the heavenly banquet.

Practical Atheism

There are always a few people who loudly claim that they are atheists. They do not respond to the opportunity of God's rule in their life because they do not believe. But there are many more of us claiming to believe in God but practicing a quiet, practical atheism. That is, living lives as though there were no God. We organize our lives and quietly give our time, ability, and influence to a plan of life not centered in God and his power.

"His real problem was not his riches but that he restructured reality by putting things in the place of God."

In reviewing the parable of the rich man and his barns, we must be careful that we do not indict the rich foolish man because he was rich! His real problem was not his riches but that he restructured reality by putting things in the place of God. In the Bible this is called idolatry. In our society of "buy," "go," "eat," and "wear," our competitive greed and self-centeredness may be showing. God calls for action, for a change in our lives. Accumulation and consumption are foolish. Living life as though possessions are central is even more foolish. "The fool says in his heart, 'There is no God' " (Ps. 14:1).

The practical atheism of our secular culture is based on these assumptions:

1. Things give your life meaning.
2. If you want to make it in life, look out for number one.
3. Ethics and morals are merely relative.
4. The only dependable things are those you can see and touch.
5. Death is a mystery that we don't understand.

These presuppositions of secularism keep us busy grubbing away at "making a living," while forgetting God. What will it take to get our attention to the fact that God is primary to our personal lives?

The Dark Midnights of Life

Many of us live our lives from one crisis to the next. Certainly, crises come into everyone's life— emotional depression, financial failure, disease, divorce, death of a loved one. I know of no life that is really free of crises.

Since life itself is a crisis that threatens us, what shall we do? Shall we try pills or positive thinking? Jesus recommends to us the behaviour of the unjust steward. Facing a severe crisis, he took prudent action. He knew everything was at

111

stake. Jesus recommends bold, resolute, and strong actions that will lead us to accept the rule of God and will lead us out of the midnight of our lives.

Our Greatest Need

The heaviest weight and the greatest burden that I have ever personally felt is my own need for forgiveness. I know of nothing as devastating, as ever-present, or as harmful to the human spirit as guilt. It is the universal disease from which we all suffer: "For all have sinned and fall short of the glory of God" (Rom.3:23).

Yet, God invites you and me to a wedding banquet—to a time of fellowship, joy, and celebration. With his invitation comes "the royal robe" of forgiveness. In both the Old and New Testaments, a garment symbolizes the redeemed community (Is. 61:10; Rev. 3:4,5,18).[9] God, full of grace and loving kindness, offers to you and me his royal robe of forgiveness. It must be worn to enter the banquet hall. Forgiven people will sit at the King's banquet table. No longer gripped in spiritual paralysis because we are forgiven and cleaned, we are able to celebrate joyously.

We must act because of what God offers us. Salvation is a free gift of God. One day he will come and scrutinize the garments that you and I wear. Will he see our torn, tattered, and dirty robes of guilt, fear, and loneliness? Or will God see us wearing his fresh, clean robe of forgiveness? Which will it be for you? The rule of God calls for you to respond.

[1] Martin E.P. Seligman, "Fall Into Helplessness," *Psychology Today* (June, 1973), pp. 43-48.

[2] John M'Clintock and James Strong, "Store-house," *Cyclopaedia of Biblical, Theological and Ecclesiastical Literature*, Vol. 9 (New York: Harper and Brothers, 1891), p. 1049.

[3] Joachim Jeremias, *Rediscovering The Parables* (New York: Charles Scribners Sons, 1966), p. 130.

[4] George A. Buttrick, ed., "Barn," *The Interpreter's Dictionary of the Bible*, Vol. 1 (Nashville: Abingdon Press, 1962), p. 356.

[5] C.U. Wolf, "Steward, Stewardship," *The Interpreter's Dictionary of the Bible*, Vol. 4, p. 443.

[6] M'Clintock and Strong, "Steward," *Cyclopaedia of Biblical, Theological and Ecclesiastical Literature*, Vol. 9, p. 1020.

[7] K.C. Pillai, *Light Through An Eastern Window* (New York: Stellar and Sons, 1963), p. 14.

[8] Ibid, pp. 14-15.

[9] Jeremias, op. cit., p. 150.

Expectant Living 8

A family went to worship one Sunday, and it was the first time that their children had ever seen Christians take the Lord's Supper. The children had seen the large table on which were placed the unleavened bread and the fruit of the vine. They had also noticed the engraved words "This do in remembrance of me" together with a small cross in the center of the words. As they were going home, one of the chidlren asked, "Daddy, what is that plus sign on the communion table?"

The New Testament asserts that Christianity is built around "a plus sign"—the cross of Jesus. The cross is the symbol of God's power, the heart of the message of the church (1 Cor. 1:18-25).

. . . The New Testament church could never be a proud, conquering church as the world understands those terms. It must remain the church of the suffering servant, a martyr church. It had no way but Christ's way: to drink of his cup (Mark 10:38-39), to take up his cross (Mark 8:34) . . . But on earth they would have no victory save the servants victory—beyond the cross.[1]

How then is the church to live? What does it mean to live as the "servant" church? What is it like to walk the way of the cross? Several of the parables of Jesus answer these questions. Not all of the parables of Christ are responses to criticism; several take us down the way of the cross that we may see more clearly the life and victory of "a plus sign."

Towers And War

Towers have had a long history in the fortification of cities in the Middle East. A tower might serve several purposes: to defend a city wall, a gate, or a strategic corner in the city wall; to observe and to attack another city; to serve as a small fortress or alarm post along a strategic area; to protect fields, vineyards, and flocks.[2]

If the work of Herod the Great is an indication of the type of walls and towers built in Palestine, the cost in material and man power must have been awesome. Even today one may see part of the massive wall, 150 feet high and stones more than 20 feet in length.[3]

Ancient armies ranged in size from a small bank of troops to the well-organized legions of the Romans. In the ninth century B.C., Amaziah built an army of 300,000 chosen men of Judah and Benjamin (2 Chron. 25). Throughout the Old Testament, God prepared his people for military conflict. On numerous occasions he had the Israelites

116

send out scouts, who would determine the size, location, and strategy of the enemy. According to the military census taken of Israel at the time of the Exodus (Num. 1), the number of infantry included something over 603,000. By the time of the New Testament, the Romans showed a military genius in their organization, battle strategies, and transportation of troops. Roman military history includes examples of intelligence, of scouting out the enemy in order to determine his strengths and capabilities.[4]

Tower Builders and Kings At War
(Luke 14:28-32)

During the early pastoral ministry of Jesus, he was extremely popular. His healing hand and his comforting message drew followers by the thousands. One day as large crowds were following Jesus, he spoke to them about one of the key prerequisites of discipleship by using two simple parables.

A man decided to build a tower. First, he drew his plans for the tower. Then, he dug down into the earth and began to construct the foundation. He placed large rocks in the ground and built the tower's foundation on them. Soon workmen were busy building it. As people of the city passed by, they could see a tower going up. Then something strange occurred. The carpenters and stonemasons quit coming to the site. Soon the place was vacant. The only thing visible was the foundation. The people of the town began to come by. They told their friends, "I want you to go out with me to see this tower. It's all of a foundation high." And they began to scoff, ridicule, and mock the builder. It seems the builder forgot one thing: he forgot to estimate the cost of building his tower. When he started, he had not thought about the cost in materials and labor to construct his tower.

Then Jesus turned to the multitudes and reminded them that this is why they must count the cost of discipleship. "And anyone who does not carry his cross and follow me cannot be my disciple" (Luke 14:27).

To point out the cost of discipleship in another way, Jesus told a second parable.

A king decided that he was powerful enough, had enough troops, and had enough ammunition to defeat his enemy. So he began to mobilize his troops. He trained them and mobilized all of his equipment, but he forgot something. He forgot to estimate the strength of his enemy. He lacked intelligence regarding his enemy's strength. At the last minute he had to make a change. Instead of thinking in terms of war, he had to think in terms of peace. And he had to send a delegation to draw up a peace treaty with his enemy.

So Jesus reminded the multitudes, who were following him like those who climb on the bandwagon of a popular movement: "In the same way, any of you who does not give up everything he has cannot be my disciple" (Luke 14:33). Self-testing is crucial to discipleship. One must count the cost of following Jesus Christ.

But both these parables suggest a second qualification for "expectant living."

Demon Possession

Demon possession frequently occurred in New Testament times. It was not at all uncommon for Jesus and his disciples to meet and deal with demon-possessed persons. Jesus differentiated between those who were emotionally ill and those who were actually possessed by demons. In treatment or therapy of those possessed with demons, he commanded the demon to leave the possessed person (Mark 6:13; Luke 13:32). Demon possession would apparently bring to a person's life violent and horrible results, such as blindness. It does not seem to be clear just how demons came to live within a person. The phenomenon of demon possession continued beyond the ministry of Jesus into the days of the early church (Acts 16:18). The New Testament offers the option of the Holy Spirit in a person's life, rather than an evil spirit.[5]

The Unclean Spirit *(Luke 11:24-26)*

Having just driven an evil spirit from a demon-possessed man, Jesus used the miracle to launch one of his parables. The point of the parable was to stress a quality of "expectant living."

There was once a man who was possessed of an evil spirit. The demon wreaked havoc through this man's life, turning him into nothing but a house of wickedness and a shattered human being. Finally, this demon left the man and went out into a desert area, where he could hide in the caves. While the demon was out in the wilderness, he found no person in which to live. There was nothing for him to do in the desert, so he decided to return to the man in whom he for-

merly lived. When he got back to that man's life, however, he found that the man had completely cleaned out his life. Everything was in order and in its proper place. But the demon saw it as an opportunity, not as a rebuke. He went and got seven other evil spirits, and they all came and made their place with him in this man's life.

Perhaps Jesus paused and looked into the eyes of his audience before completing the parable with these words: "And the final condition of that man was worst than the first." Jesus taught that it is not enough for a person simply to subtract the negative—he must also add the positive to his life. Every person is ruled by either evil or good. A religion that only subtracts evil and does not fill up a life with the good is only part "Christian." To turn one's life over to *Jesus as Lord* and allow him to be the new master of one's existence is the essence of Christianity.

Overseers

In the New Testament times there were two classes of overseers or stewards. First, there was the overseer whose function was that of "guardian," one entrusted with the care of another person. Second, there was the overseer who functioned as a manager, administering the responsibilities of the owner. Apparently, the concept of "delegated responsibility" was at the heart of the function of both classes of stewards.[6]

Steward With Supervision (*Luke 12:42-46*) and The Talents (*Matt. 25:14-30*)

In speaking to his disciples concerning the way

a person lives his life in the kingdom, Jesus taught them with another parable.

A man, who owned a large estate, decided to make a long journey. So he called his steward and placed him in charge of all the other servants. The man failed to tell the steward, though, when he would return. Thus, the steward reasoned to himself, "I'm in charge now. I can do anything I want." He began to beat the other servants, a practice the master had never used. The steward abused his master's trust by holding a lot of drunken feasts and generally ignoring his duties. Then without warning, the master returned in the middle of the night and found the results of his misplaced trust: his possessions had been abused and his servants had been beaten and injured. The master, therefore, punished his steward severely.

Then Jesus concluded, "You must watch and stay ready for the coming of your master." To make another point concerning responsible behavior, Jesus told another parable.

There was a certain man of vast wealth, who was called away from home for a long period of time. Before he left, he decided that he would entrust his investments to three of his stewards. As a good businessman, he wanted his wealth to reproduce itself. So he called the first steward and gave him five talents—a considerable fortune even by modern standards. Then, he called in the second trusted steward and gave him two talents—still a large amount of money. Next, he called in a third servant and gave him one talent.

He gave to each of these servants according to what he thought each could handle, according to their ability. And then he went on his journey.

The first steward, who had five talents, invested those five talents. He took a risk, and it paid handsome dividends—the five doubled to ten talents. The two-talent man looked at his options, took a risk, invested wisely, and also doubled his investment. The one-talent man sat down, looked at his options, and thought to himself: "I could squander it, but I don't want to do that. Or I could sink it in an investment, but that's risky. And I know about my master. He expects profit. I might even lose the one talent I've got. I know what I'll do. I'll dig a hole and hide the talent. That way I won't lose it. And when my master comes back, I'll dig it up and present it to him."

One day the master returned. He called in the man who had been given five talents and was presented with ten talents. The master said, "Well done servant. You're going to share in my wealth for you have used my wealth responsibly and faithfully."

Then, he called in the second man, who presented him not with two talents but with four, and said, "Well done; you are faithful. You used my investments, and you used them well. You're going to share in my wealth."

Finally, he called in the man who had buried his talent. The steward explained, "I know you don't like to lose money. So you're going to be delighted to know that I didn't lose your money while you were gone. I went out, dug a hole, and hid it. And here it is, just what you gave me before you left." The master dismissed him, saying, "You will not share in my wealth because you are an unfaithful servant. You did not take a risk, nor the opportunity I gave you."

"... Jesus calls for responsible living in the present as the best preparation for the future."

In his teachings, Jesus stressed that one of the qualities of "expectant living" is *responsible behavior*. To live in the kingdom is to be given a position of trust. God calls upon those in the kingdom to not abuse this trust. "From everyone who has been given much, much will be demanded; and from the one who has been entrusted with much, much more will be asked," claims Jesus (Luke 12:48b). So important to "expectant living" is responsible behavior that it is the key to preparing for the future. No need for panic, astrology, or doom—instead Jesus calls for responsible living in the present as the best preparation for the future.

Costly Discipleship

We must consider and count the cost when we are thinking about the rule of God in our lives. When Jesus said this, he was talking about something much more than being a member of some religious group or attending an occasional church service.

If you and I are to follow a religion that has cost God his one and only Son and that has cost

Jesus his very life's blood, then it is going to cost us, too! For Jesus calls us to completely commit ourselves to following him as our Saviour and our Lord. He wants to be absolutely certain that we do not become counterfeit Christians. "If anyone would come after me, he must deny himself and take up his cross daily and follow me. For whoever wants to save his life will lose it, but whoever loses his life for me will save it" (Luke 9:23-24).

But what is your "cross"? What is it that you and I must give up if we are to be totally committed to Christ? Is there something you highly value that may stand in the way of your relationship with God? Are not you and I required, as Abraham was, to give up our "Isaac"? Is not our own personal cross our own personal will and desires that intersect with the will of God for our lives?

If you and I are going to take up our cross "daily" and going to keep counting the cost in our life, what kinds of things must we do? What does it mean to "deny" ourself in order to "follow Jesus"?

Spiritual Changes

Becoming a follower of Jesus Christ is not only a matter of commitment, nor only a matter of subtracting vices from one's life, but also a matter of adding to one's life. At our baptism, we receive "the gift of the Holy Spirit" (Acts 2:38). When God's Spirit begins to give birth to our spirit, changes begin to take place. These changes are *spiritual*. "The wind blows wherever it pleases.

You may hear its sound, but you cannot tell where it comes from or where it is going. So it is with everyone born of the Spirit" (John 3:8).

As we sweep what is evil out of our houses, God's Holy Spirit begins to add that which is beautiful and fine. "But the fruit of the Spirit is love, joy, peace, patience, kindness, goodness, faithfulness, gentleness and self-control" (Gal. 5:22-23a).

So "expectant living" brings a new master—God's Holy Spirit, who comes into our lives and becomes obvious in our daily actions and attitudes.

Entrusted to Us

"Expectant living" includes using responsibly the trust God has given to us. As stewards of God, who do not know when the return of the master will be, we are called to live lives of obedient trust.

"We don't decide whether God will join us in our mission but whether we will join him in his mission."

Consider what God has entrusted to you and me! First, he has entrusted us with his word to use in our lives. We are not to abuse it. Think of what's been done to abuse the word of God over the last two thousand years. Often it is the sad story of using the word of God to frighten, scare, and justify some of the strangest views and religious ceremonies! To be responsible stewards of

God will take serious, personal study of the word of God, seeing it as an ever-deepening well from which to draw the water of life. One does not approach it with the attitude of religious self-righteousness but with a spirit of humility and openness.

God has also entrusted to us his precious promises. As anchors for our spirits, his promises give us a solid foundation of security and assurance. The promises of God are very specific, clear, and practical. They deal with significant areas of our lives, such as worrying, guilt, the future, marriage and family life, and our own emotional health. A strong belief in the promises of God characterize a life of responsible trust.

God entrusts to his people the possibility of joining him in his mission. God's mission to planet earth is tied to "expectant living." God calls upon his people to carry out the mission and life of Jesus. We don't decide whether God will join us in *our* mission but whether we will join him in *his* mission. As servants entrusted with the mission of God, we are called to be

> . . . a royal priesthood, a holy nation, a people belonging to God, that you may declare the praises of him who called you out of darkness into his wonderful light."

1 Peter 2:9

When we stay close to the message and mission of Jesus, we behave responsibly as faithful stewards. We work out of a position of trust. God has placed his mission in our hands. We dare not fail!

So Jesus marks kingdom business by three distinguishing characteristics:

* Total commitment after counting the cost.
* Turning life over to the lordship of Christ and the Holy Spirit.
* A responsible behavior, using what God has given us.

Let us live expectantly, for no one knows the day or the hour when our master will return.

---

[1] John Bright, *The Kingdom of God* (Nashville: Abingdon Press, 1953), pp. 236-237.

[2] Merrill C. Tenney, ed., *The Zondervan Pictorial Bible Dictionary* (Grand Rapids: Zondervan Publishing House, 1963), p. 861; J.D. Douglas, ed., *The New Bible Dictionary* (Grand Rapids: William B. Eerdmans Publishing Co., 1975), pp. 436-439.

[3] Ibid., pp. 436-438; Tenney, op. cit., p. 861.

[4] Tenney, op. cit., pp. 72-73.

[5] For an interesting article on "demon possession," see Douglas, op. cit., pp. 1010-1012.

[6] Douglas, op. cit., p. 1216.

Why Should I Care? 9

In many ways Jesus Christ was the simplest person who ever lived! His birth was without the glitter and glamour that royalty normally attracts. He lived an uncomplicated life among peasant people in the despised village of Nazareth. Jesus never traveled more than two hundred miles from his birth place (except on one occasion when his parents took him to Egypt to escape the purge of Bethlehem). By the standards of Greek and Roman education, he was untrained. He did not own any property and wore very plain clothes. By the standards of his society, he was considered a failure.

The simplicity of Jesus still confuses those who look for sophistication. His plainness still confounds those who believe that understanding is the same thing as intelligence.

Jesus Christ is the most profound person who ever lived! He spoke of God and life in simple language, yet understood, perceived, and accurately saw into the human situation. Jesus didn't quote the various rabbis to support his statements, for his statements were valid at face value. Thus, he amazed people because "he taught as one who had authority" (Matt. 7:28-29).

Both the simplicity and depth of Jesus were evident when he spoke of the nature of his kingdom to Pilate:

> Jesus said, "My kingdom is not of this world. If it were, my servants would fight to prevent my arrest by the Jews. But now my kingdom is from another place." "You are a king, then!" said Pilate. Jesus answered, "You are right in saying I am a king. In fact, for this reason I was born, and for this I came into the world, to testify to the truth. Everyone on the side of truth listens to me."
>
> John 18:36-37

Since the kingdom of God is not a political-social state, how do you know if you're in the kingdom? How can you be sure that the rule of God lives in you? Jesus has answered these questions in two popular and practical parables: one is the Good Samaritan; the other is the Rich Man and Lazarus.

Priests, Levites, And Samaritans

The road from Jerusalem to Jericho was known for its danger and covered seventeen miles. Those treacherous miles of the lonely, narrow road twists through the Judean hills down to Jericho. In ancient days, just as in modern times, robberies frequently took place on the Jericho road. It was in a time where little value was given to human life; and it was not unusual for a person to be found on the Jericho road stripped, beaten, and half alive.

Priests were the descendants of Aaron and, beginning with the time of David, were organized into twenty-four orders (1 Chron. 24:1-19). Even though priests were assigned to various cities, such as Jericho, each order of the priesthood served in the temple two weeks of each year.

The sons of Levi were consecrated as helpers for the priests. These Levites were divided into three families, each having specific duties. The principal function of the Levites was in the rituals of cleansing and dedication (Num. 8:5ff).[1]

Why, then, would a priest not help a person in need? He may have been unsure whether the victim was dead or alive, and ritual forbade a priest to touch a dead body (Lev. 21:11). Of course, the priest simply might have been in a great hurry— too busy to reach out to human needs! Whatever may have been his reason, the Levite did not reach out to the needs of the man in the ditch. As Lightfoot stresses, "Thus the priest and the Levite by their occupations recognize the claims of God, but in their lives they fail to recognize the claim of humanity."[2]

A history of bitterness and resentment marked the relationship between Jews and Samaritans. In 722 B.C. the Assyrians deported the leading citizens of Israel. Those Jews whom the Assyrians left in the land intermarried with non-Jews. During the period of the rebuilding of the temple, the Samaritans opposed the Jews, perhaps only for political reasons. By the time of Nehemiah, the feelings between the Jews and Samaritans were running strong and deep. By the time of Jesus, feelings were at an all time low. ("Between A.D. 6 and 9 Samaritans scattered bones in the Jerusalem temple during a certain Passover."³) With this desecration, animosity intensified. Jews called Samaritans "dogs" and would cross the Jordan River on foot rather than travel through Samaria. Proud of their racial heritage, Jews looked upon the Samaritans as traitors and heretics. What a shock to a Jew, then, that Jesus would choose a Samaritan as a person of compassion.

The Good Samaritan *(Luke 10:25-37)*

A sharp lawyer tested Jesus by engaging him in a philosophical discussion on the bounds and limits of being a "neighbor." Wanting to justify himself, the lawyer asked Jesus, "And who is my neighbor?" In reply, Jesus told him a story.

A man traveled the seventeen miles between Jerusalem and Jericho. As he traveled along his way, robbers rushed out from the ditch and behind the rocks. They stole his money and his clothes and beat him up, leaving him almost dead. After a while a priest happened to be going down the same road. He heard moans of pain, anguish, and cries for help. He saw the half-alive man lying in the ditch beside the road. Do you know what the priest did? He kept on walking! After a while a Levite, a helper in the temple, came upon the beaten, half-dead man. He, too, kept on walking. Traveling the same seventeen miles, a Samaritan came upon the half-alive Jew. This Samaritan, however, saw the

injured man's urgent needs and was moved with compassion. He stopped and got down into the ditch beside the man. He disinfected the wounds and carefully bandaged them. He then lifted the man upon his donkey and tenderly held him all the way to the Jericho inn. The next day he took out two days wages and gave them to the inn-keeper saying, "Look after him; and when I return, I will reimburse you for any extra expense you may have."

Which of these people was a true "neighbor"? The expert in the law apparently couldn't bring himself to say the word "Samaritan" and so responded, "The one who had mercy on him." Jesus replied, "You go and do likewise."

Beggars And Rich People

In the Old Testament, relieving the need of a beggar was considered a personal virtue. The New Testament also has a great deal to say about material possessions. Since poor people tend to look beyond themselves for guidance and direction in their lives, they were attracted to Jesus in great numbers (Luke 4:18). Through his message and his life, Jesus stressed the importance of meeting the needs of the poor, of those in need.

The contrast between rich and poor was vivid in Jesus' time. The scene of a crippled, diseased and hungry beggar was a tragic but common one. Jesus could well have seen street dogs licking sores of a beggar sitting at the gate of a rich man's mansion. In ancient times, those who ate sumptuously at a rich man's table would dip pieces of bread in their dish, wipe their hands on the

bread, and throw them under the table.[4] Beggars
often scrambled for these pieces of bread.

The rich lived in sharp contrast to the beggar in
the street. Playboy types were known in the time
of Christ—those who surrounded themselves
with all the luxury of high living. Often wearing
Egyptian "royal linen" and purple robes of honor
and wealth, a rich man had the finest of everything.[5] With his wealth came all the expressions
of fine living, along with the temptation to depend upon himself rather than God. After all, he
had contacts; he knew his way around; he could
solve his own problems.

The Rich Man And Lazarus *(Luke 16:19-31)*

Jesus told a parable about wealth and depen-
dence upon God.

There was a wealthy man who dressed in the
finest clothes, ate from a bountiful table, lived in
a very comfortable house with all the luxuries,
and spent his time satisfying his own desires. He
had great fortune and used it for himself. But at
the doorstep of his mansion laid a beggar named
Lazarus. He was diseased, crippled, and so hungry that he wished to eat the pieces of bread that
the rich man threw under his table. Roaming
street dogs came and licked the running sores of
Lazarus' body.

But the time came when both of them died.
The beggar took his place with the righteous, but
the rich man took his place with those separated
from God's presence. The rich man begged Abraham, who was beside Lazarus, for compassion
and fortune. But Abraham replied, "Remember

that in your lifetime you had good things, but you lacked kindness and compassion. On earth Lazarus received bad things, but his humility and faithfulness are now rewarded." The rich man, then, pleaded for an opportunity for his five brothers to be warned concerning eternity. Abraham replied, "They have Moses and the prophets; and if they will not listen to them, they'll not be convinced if someone rises from the dead."

Jesus taught his disciples that this story points to the eternal destiny of anyone who shows the absence of God's rule in his own life. To be surrounded with abundance and luxury and not be moved with empathy for those in need—this is to miss the point about life in the kingdom. Lack of compassion, pity, and feeling for those in deep need demonstrates the total absence of the rule of God in one's life.

Kingdom Ethics

In order to bring us back into a relationship with God, Jesus must sweep away the religious and cultural interpretations, formalities, and ceremonies and must paint clearly the picture of how God rules us. In these two parables Jesus becomes very practical. As Lightfoot comments,

> It gets down to the bottom of what Christianity really is. There is not room for pious platitudes and hair-splitting definitions, no place for Christianity in the abstract or for a religion to be seen of man. With one scene that flashes upon the screen, Jesus compels us to see that *Christianity is a way of living.*[6]

The ethic of Jesus must translate into action. "After all," writes D. Martyn Lloyd-Jones, "The Law was not meant to be praised, it was meant to be practiced. Our Lord did not preach the Sermon on the Mount in order that you and I might comment upon it, but in order that we might carry it out."[7]

What are the *ethics* of the kingdom? Are not the ethical concerns of those ruled by God the identical concerns of Jesus Christ? Would not those who follow Jesus today carry on his ethical concerns? But the ethics of Jesus only make sense to those who are in *submission* to the lordship of Christ! So as Jesus fed the hungry, clothed the naked, and ministered to prisoners, he demonstrated the great *inward* concern of God for the human situation. The Bible does not claim that Jesus came to establish a series of social programs designed to improve or reform society. To reduce the good news of the kingdom of God into a series of social reformations in the non-Christian world is the same as asking people to accept the ethics of Jesus without accepting his rulership in their lives.

"The word of God does not call upon us to make a choice between social concern or personal salvation. It calls for both!"

But at precisely this point, some are tempted to walk away from the issue of human concern without feeling a sense of responsibility for the world's needs. Many religious people today still call Jesus "Lord, Lord" (Matt. 7:21-23) and lift his name up in respect and worship, yet show no relationship to him by ministering to the needs of others. The word of God does not call upon us to make a choice between social concern or personal salvation. It calls for both! We are truly "Christian" only if our salvation leads us to serve others. It is when we personally respond to the lordship of Christ and allow God to rule our hearts that we then begin to serve the needs of our fellowman. So God says throughout his word that his religion hangs on two commandments: (1) to personally love and serve God, and (2) to love and serve one's fellowman (Deut. 6:4-9).

To "love one's neighbor" is to serve *anyone* who needs help. So the range of application for the ethic of the kingdom includes everyone. Unconditional love, which is learned from the greatest lover, will cause us to become servants prepared to be exploited, to be used, and to show deep feeling for those in need. People still lie "beside the road" and at our "gate." Consider the hungry, the orphans, the disenfranchised, the sick, the jobless, the prisoner, the emotionally ill, the unguided youth, the aged, the unmarried pregnant women, and the dying. So let's not miss the point of our faith: *service to our fellowman comes out of a life ruled by God.* "In everything, do to others what you would have them do to you, for this sums up the Law and the Prophets" (Matt. 7:12). "To obey this commandment a man must become a new man with a new centre to his life. . . ."[8]

Christianity or Culture

Kingdom business is to be concerned about the

real needs of real people! The nature of the Lord's kingdom is not political or social. So Jesus says, "My kingdom is not of this world" (John 18:36). The kingdom of God runs counter to the kingdom of the world when it comes to ethics.

Our culture says, "Think of your self first . . . Look after number one; if you don't no one else will . . . Protect your rights and privileges . . . Just don't get caught." But the way of Christ shows that an ethic rooted in self is like the priest and Levite, who passed by human concern "on the other side of the road" or like the rich man who showed no concern for Lazarus.

In direct contrast to culture, Christ says, "Deny yourself . . . Serve others . . . Whatever you did for one of the least of these brothers of mine, you did for me."

Beside The Road

Jesus promises us that when we lay our lives down in service to God and our fellowman, *then* we truly find life.

> I tell you the truth, unless a kernel of wheat falls to the ground and dies, it remains only a single seed. But if it dies, it produces many seeds. The man who loves his life will lose it, while the man who hates his life in this world will keep it for eternal life.
>
> John 12:24-25

Sure it's hard! It's incredibly hard! No one in scripture ever said it would be easy. To translate into daily life the ethical concerns of the kingdom is to be beside the roads of life and out at the gates of life, to be among real people who have real needs. It's to lay our lives down, wash feet, identify with the pain of people, and find our life.

> We always carry around in our body the death of Jesus, so that the life of Jesus may also be revealed in our body. For we who are alive are always being given over to death for Jesus' sake, so that his life may be revealed in our mortal body. So then, death is at work in us, but life is at work in you.
>
> 2 Corinthians 4:10-12

A Process And The Product

How shall we carry out the ethic of the kingdom? How shall we serve the *real* needs of *real* people?

"When God comes to rule in the heart of a person, the ethics of Jesus are worked out in his daily life."

The Bible describes the ethic of the kingdom as a process which is shaping us into a final product—the image of Christ. This process is marked by three characteristics:

(1) It is an ethic of *specifics*, not generalities.

(2) It is an ethic of *action*, not apathy.

(3) It is an ethic of *compassion*, not self-centeredness.

When God comes to rule in the heart of a person, the ethics of Jesus are worked out in his daily life. Satan tempts us to grow weary of the process that God uses to shape us into the image of God. C.S. Lewis describes the process:

When I was a child I often had toothaches, and I knew that if I went to my mother she would give me something which would deaden the pain for that night and let me get to sleep. But I did not go to my mother—at least, not till the pain became very bad. And the reason I did not go was this. I did not doubt she would give me the aspirin; but I knew she would take me to the dentist the next morning. I could not get what I wanted out of her without getting something more, which I did not want. I wanted immediate relief from pain, but I could not get it without having my teeth set permanently right. And I knew those dentists; I knew they started fiddling about with all sorts of other teeth which had not yet begun to ache. They would not let sleeping dogs lie; if you gave them an inch they took an ell.

Now, if I may put it that way, Our Lord is like the dentists. If you give Him an inch, He will take an ell. Dozens of people go to Him to be cured of some one particular sin which they are ashamed of (like masturbation or physical cowardice) or which is obviously spoiling daily life (like bad temper or drunkenness). Well, He will cure it all right: but He will not stop there. That may be all you asked; but if once you call Him in, He will give you the full treatment.

That is why He warned people to "count the cost" before becoming Christians. "Make no mistake," He says, "if you let me, I will make you perfect. The moment you put yourself in my hands, that is what you are in for. Nothing less, or other, than that. You have free will, and if you choose, you can push Me away. But if you do not push Me away, understand that I am going to see this job through. Whatever suffering it may cost you in your earthly life, whatever inconceivable purification it may cost you after death, and whatever it costs Me, I will never rest, nor let you rest, until you are literally perfect—until my Father can say without reservation that He is well pleased with you, as He said He was well pleased with me. This I can do and will do. But I will not do anything less.[9]

These two parables call us to think of others first and to serve their needs. The process of self-denial, of laying down our personal lives in the service of the needs of other people and of giving ourselves over to loving God and our fellowman, is a most difficult and at times a very painful process. But we can thank God, the Potter, for shaping us into the very image he has in mind. In the end, we won't even recognize what we look like, for we will look like Christ!

---

[1] For additional background reading on priests and Levites, see D.A. Hubbard, "Priests and Levites," *The New Bible Dictionary* (Grand Rapids: William B. Eerdmans Publishing Company, 1975), pp. 1028-1034.

[2] Neil R. Lightfoot, *Lessons From The Parables* (Grand Rapids: Baker Book House, 1965), p. 65.

[3] Hubbard, op. cit., p. 1132.

[4] Joachim Jeremias, *Rediscovering The Parables* (New York: Charles Scribner's Sons, 1966), p. 146.

[5] F.C. Fensham, "Linen," *The New Bible Dictionary*, pp. 740-741; Lightfoot, op. cit., p. 134.

[6] Ibid., pp. 65-66.

[7] D. Martyn Lloyd-Jones, *Studies in the Sermon on the Mount*, Vol. 2 (Grand Rapids: William B. Eerdmans Publishing Co., 1967), p. 211.

[8] William Barclay, *The Gospel of Matthew*, Vol. 1 (Philadelphia: The Westminster Press, 1959), p. 281.

[9] C.S. Lewis, *Mere Christianity* (New York: Macmillan Co., 1958), pp. 157-158.

Why Do I Trust Whom I Trust? 10

The statement, "In God we trust," stamped on our coins is a remarkable one. It is actually a profound claim, an assertion, a desire, a hope. The power of this statement lies in its claim: this nation claims to rely upon God. Whether we do or not may be a real question, but the word "trust" is one we need to examine carefully.

"Trust" is difficult to come by. Our society seems to function on fine print, exceptions to the rule, unfulfilled promises, and half-truths. Children naturally trust until they are taught to mistrust. I understand "trust" to be *reliance on someone in a risk-taking situation.* If your child jumps from a high place into your arms, your child expresses "trust" in you in a risk-taking moment. We are constantly told that it is difficult to *trust* someone other than ourselves:

"If you want something done right, do it yourself!"

"I'd rather do it myself!"

"Have it your way!"

Our world admires and respects the trait of "self-reliance" or "independence." We are told we can trust only ourselves when confronting the unknowns and crises of living.

In a world with a credibility problem, how can I trust anyone other than myself? At this point, Jesus presents us the option of the kingdom of God, the rule of God for our lives. He presents the kingdom of God to us like a jewel, turning it a few degrees at a time so that we might see it at different angles. To understand what we are seeing, we must grasp the meaning of the parables of Jesus.

Pharisees, Tax Collectors, And Prayer

At the time of Jesus, three groups made up Judaism—the Essenes, the Sadducees, and the Pharisees. Of the three, the Pharisees were the most prominent. They possibly had their origin at the time of the Maccabees and were also known as the *Chasidim* or "pious ones." Pharisees believed that *they* were the only "loyal ones to God," a loyalty that was based upon these distinctive beliefs:

* God controls and governs history.
* God raises the dead and brings them into a future life, where they are rewarded or punished according to their life on earth.
* Spirits and angels exist.
* Only the true sons of Israel, those loyal to God, enjoy a special, close relationship with him.[1]

The Pharisees distinguished themselves by several characteristics, all of which led to *self-trust*.

First, they possessed a legalistic purity, devoting themselves to the Jewish law and to a strict interpretation of it. These interpretations were handed down from one generation to another. They bound their interpretations on Jewish life and considered their interpretations part of the will of God. From tithing one-tenth of their garden vegetables to taking down the body of Christ before the Sabbath day, the Pharisees insisted on rigorous keeping of the law. For them, the essence of religion lay in knowledge and obedience of the law. But Jesus judged them because the corresponding *spirituality* was missing from their daily life: "For I tell you that unless your righteousness surpasses that of the Pharisees and the teachers of the law, you will certainly not enter the kingdom of heaven" (Matt. 5:20). Jesus has given us a description of Pharisaic legalism— religion built on self-trust. His verdict: " . . . But do not do what they do, for they do not practice what they preach" (Matt. 23:3).

A second characteristic of Phariseeism was its profound respect for custom and tradition. Pharisees developed a strong confidence in the Jewish "oral law," the customs and traditions of the religion. By the time of Jesus, the keeping of their traditions had built a wall between them and God. Jesus challenged them:

> And why do you break the command of God for the sake of your tradition? For God said, "Honor your father and mother," and, "Anyone

who curses his father or mother must be put to death." But you say that if a man says to his father or his mother, "Whatever help you might otherwise have received from me is a gift devoted to God," he is not to "honor his father" with it. Thus you nullify the word of God for the sake of your tradition.

Matthew 15:3-6

The keeping of traditions led to self-satisfaction. While Jesus did not encourage disobedience to the law, he showed no regard for a religion based on self-satisfaction.

"Jews despised and degraded tax collectors as members of the criminal community."

A third characteristic of Phariseeism was intolerance. Seeing themselves as the *only* "loyal ones," they exhibited prejudice towards those different from themselves. They one-sidedly emphasized the external acts of religion: formal prayers (Matt. 6:5f), public fasting (Matt. 6:16-18), public offerings (Matt. 6:1-4), and wearing robes with special borders with scriptures (Matt. 23:5). They worked diligently to bring others to their views (Matt. 23:15). Pharisees prided themselves in their noninvolvement with others, especially bad people. Their intolerance and their legalism enslaved them and closed them up to possibilities for change, which gave them justification for killing Jesus.

Tax collectors never have been the objects of

great affection; and in the time of Christ, people especially hated them. Caesar had decreed that the taxes of Judea were to be levied by tax collectors in Judea and paid directly to the Roman government.[2] Jews who hired out to Rome to collect taxes were considered traitors, employees of a foreign power. Jewish tax collectors would pay in advance an amount stipulated by Rome for the right to collect taxes in a particular locality. Any taxes they could collect from fellow Jews above this stipulated amount would be their profit. Jewish sources considered tax collectors as robbers and associated them with oppression and injustice. Tax collectors had no civil rights and were "disqualified from holding communal office, even from giving testimony in a Jewish court."[3] Jews despised and degraded tax collectors as members of the criminal community. "Against such unscrupulous oppressors every kind of deception was allowed; goods might be declared to be votive offerings or a person could pass his slave as his son."[4] Jesus' association with tax collectors brought him into disrepute with the religious leaders.

The law prescribed prayer night and day whenever the needs of the people called for prayer. Formal prayer might be made at the same time as temple services, which was in the morning and in the evening. Three times a day was recognized as appropriate (Ps. 55:17; Dan. 6:10), with the sixth hour (Acts 10:9) and the ninth hour (Acts 3:1; 10:3, 30) especially noted.[5] Temple prayers were usually oral, spoken aloud like reading.[6] A person might assume numerous postures in his prayer, such as standing, kneeling, prostration, bowing the head, or spreading the hands toward heaven.[7]

Pharisees And Tax Collectors *(Luke 18:9-14)*

Religion sometimes is vulnerable to those who want to trust in themselves. It occasionally attracts people who want to look up to themselves and down on others. Like Mount Ranier in the state of Washington, it looks down on everything and everything looks up to it. The paradox of it all is that even though the religion of God sometimes attracts those who rely upon themselves, they never discover how to practice the religion of God. To an audience "who were confident of their own righteousness and looked down upon everybody else," Jesus had something to say. It can be found in the parable that follows:

At the appropriate time of daily prayer, two men went up to the temple to pray. One was a Pharisee, and the other was a despised tax collector. The Pharisee chose a prominent place to pray so that others would see him and even hear his prayer. Do you know what the Pharisee prayed? He didn't thank God for God's gifts to him, but he did thank God for one thing—for himself! The Pharisee said, "God, I thank you that I'm not like other men—robbers, evil doers, adulterers—or even like this tax collector." He reminded God of things that he had never done that the tax collector had done. You know what else he prayed? He reminded God of two things that he had done that God hadn't required: he fasted *twice* a week, and he gave a tenth of *all* his

income. The prayer was a standard, a formal reminder to God of how devout the Pharisee was.

Then, the tax collector prayed. He chose a less prominent place to pray. In seclusion, he began to pray. Uncomfortable in the presence of a righteous God, the tax collector did not even look toward the direction of God. He felt nothing in himself that would recommend himself to God. And so he beat his breast saying, "God, have mercy on me, a sinner." The tax collector felt he had done all the wrong things—robbed, committed evil, been unfaithful—and needed forgiveness from a loving God. Both men went home, but only one man went home in a right relationship with God. It was not the Pharisee, who depended upon his own merits of righteousness, but the tax collector, who trusted in God for his righteousness. For everyone who trusts in himself will be humbled, but he who humbles himself and trusts in God will be exalted.

"It is in trusting, not trying, that God's rule becomes evident."

To the religiously confident Jesus declared that the rule of God would come only into the hearts of people who trusted God, not themselves. It is in trusting, not trying, that God's rule becomes evident. Humility of spirit offers hope for eternity. The paradox is that those who trust in themselves, being confident of their right relationship with God, have no relationship with him. Yet, those who recognize their need have a relationship with God. The kingdom of God, Jesus said, is able to move into a life when one is dependent, not independent.

Whom Do You Trust?

The real problem of "Phariseeism" is that religion turns sour, holiness becomes "holier than thou," and godliness becomes humanistic. Jesus constantly warns that self-righteousness keeps a person from a relationship with God. Phariseeism is a sin that is still with us as long as religious people trust in their own righteousness rather than becoming humble before God.

Who do you and I *trust*? Do we trust ourselves, our contacts with other people, our record of service of good deeds, or our material possessions? Let's spell out in detail the difference between trusting in ourselves and trusting in God.

Self-Trust
(Life is what *You* make it)

Represses guilt
Develops hypocrisy
Is sensitive to good works
Becomes defensive
Covers up failures
Asserts self
Stimulates ego
Emphasizes performance, achievement, and merit
Feels insecure
Confronts crises with panic
Manipulates, dominates, and orders
Concentrates on/remembers old habits and patterns

Protects rights and privileges
Manipulates others as objects
Leads to despair and depression

God-Trust
(Life is what *God* makes it)
Forgives guilt
Develops openness
Is sensitive to God's leading
Becomes open
Confesses failures
Denies self
Stimulates humility
Emphasizes reliance and faith
Feels boldness
Gives strength to cope with crises
Listens, asks, and suggests
Develops potential
Loses rights and privileges
Serves others as persons
Gives victory

When all the items in the column of self-trust are added together, they equal "losing life." Life is filled with the scattered remains of lives built on self. In sharp contrast, when all the items under "God-trust" are added together, they equal "finding life." So Jesus says, "The man who loves his life will lose it, while the man who hates his life in this world will keep it for eternal life" (John 12:25). Do I really see myself as being able to handle my own life, or do I see myself in need of God's mercy? The one upon whom I continually *rely* is the one I trust. Is that God or self?

A Dominating Or Submissive Spirit

The wisdom of the world calls upon you and me to assert self. It tells us that the only way to live happy and successful in the world is to dominate other people, protect ourselves, and stay very conscious of who's superior to whom. This type of "narcissim" likes what it sees! Unfortunately, hundreds of thousands of people have bought in heavily on this approach to living life. Record-breaking numbers of broken homes, desertions, and one-parent families suggest that *selfishness* is a major cause of broken family life. It causes individuals to dominate and control others and assert themselves.

"The character of God is such that he cannot work in the life of the self-righteous."

Throughout the scripture, there is one basic requirement for a person's life—"a broken spirit": "The sacrifices of God are a broken spirit; a broken and contrite heart, Oh God, you will not despise" (Ps. 51:17). The character of God is such that he cannot work in the life of the self-righteous. But he can come into the heart and life of the humble and broken-spirited person. He reaches down with understanding and compassion to the contrite of heart. This humility of spirit or submission to the will of God marks the people of God.

The gap between what we are and what we could become is not a thin line but a grand canyon. My experience tells me that it is at these very moments of awareness that God is closest to us—coming into our hearts, ruling us, and making fundamental changes in our lives. While God rejects self-righteousness, he accepts humility. Can you think of an incident in your life when you felt distant from God, but he surprised you with his closeness?

Personal Trust In God

"I tell you that this man, rather than the other, went home justified before God. For whoever exalts himself will be humbled, and he who humbles himself will be exalted." Jesus doesn't often use the word "justified." We normally think of the word as belonging to Paul and being found especially in the book of Romans. But at the conclusion of his parables, Jesus lays down the paradox of salvation:

A tax collector receives mercy.
A beggar is in Abraham's bosom.
Samaritans are accepted.
Street people are invited to the banquet.

Logic and reason would tell us the opposite: the pious and holy are accepted by God. But Jesus is putting the doctrine of justification in parable form. Justification means to enter into a state or condition of acceptance with God. And the basis of justification before God is personal trust in his mercy. It begins when a person "beats his breast and says, 'God have mercy on me, a sinner.' " So whenever one is torn apart by guilt and then trusts in God's mercy for salvation, he is " . . . justified freely by (God's) grace through the redemption that came by Christ Jesus" (Rom. 3:24).

Do we still need to hear this parable today? Are there not thousands and thousands of people, both churched and unchurched who try to come to God on the basis of their merits? Are there not many trying to square themselves with God by their duties and obligations? Are there not multitudes who do not understand that the only way that a man can go "home justified before God" is on the basis of trust in his mercy? And whenever we trust in ourselves and fall upon our faces, aren't we painfully reminded that we do not have the wisdom within ourselves to know what is best for ourselves? And are not the hardest working Christians those who have been justified by God's mercy?

You see, Jesus is saying that it's only when I see myself as unfit as a tax collector and say, "God, have mercy on me, a sinner," that I will find life. That really does make the gospel "good news"!

> The Spirit of the Lord is on me; because he has anointed me to preach good news to the poor. He has sent me to proclaim freedom for the prisoners and recovery of sight for the blind, to release the oppressed, to proclaim the year of the Lord's favor.
>
> Luke 4:18-19

The secret lies in trusting in God—just as our coins declare.

'For further information on Phariseeism, see Matthew Black, "Pharisees," *The Interpreter's Dictionary of the Bible*, Vol. 3 (Nashville: Abingdon Press, 1962), pp. 776-778; Lorman M.

Petersen, "Pharisees," *The Zondervan Pictorial Bible Dictionary* (Grand Rapids: Zondervan Publishing House, 1963), pp. 647-648.

[2] Alfred Edersheim, *The Life and Times of Jesus The Messiah*, Vol. 1 (Grand Rapids: William B. Eerdmans Publishing Co., 1953), p. 517.

[3] B.J. Bamberger, "Tax Collector," *The Interpreter's Dictionary of the Bible*, Vol. 4, p. 522.

[4] Edersheim, op. cit., Vol. 1, p. 516.

[5] C.W.F. Smith, "Prayer," *The Interpreter's Dictionary of the Bible*, Vol. 3, p. 866.

[6] Joachim Jeremias, *Rediscovering the Parables* (New York: Charles Scribner's Sons, 1966), pp. 111-112.

[7] C.W.F. Smith, op. cit., p. 866.

The King Who Cares 11

Jesus never seemed to care about the things that people normally cared about in living. Material things did not impress him. He didn't place high priority on what people thought of him, nor was he interested in making contacts that might elevate his position.

Clearly, Jesus had concerns that were different from man, and he wanted to convey and communicate these concerns. As he lived among the people, he looked for symbols in their ordinary, daily activity that convey his concerns. Even though we might never completely understand the nature of God's rule in our lives, Jesus wants us to catch a gleam, a shadow, of what the kingdom is really like in life.

As Jesus walked the streets of ancient Palestine, he saw many beggars. They would ask everyone for help, coins, or bread. Asking each person that passed by, these beggars never gave up and were ever-present.

Their persistence impressed Jesus, and he used this quality to make a point about the rule of God in a person's life.

This point is found in one of the parables Jesus told to reveal the nature of God and the nature of our communication with God.

Judges And Widows

The judges mentioned in the New Testament performed a different function from those mentioned in the Old Testament book of Judges. Israel looked up to her judges as heroes, leaders in battle, and rulers: " . . . the Lord raised up judges, who saved them out of the hands of these raiders" (Judg. 2:16). They acted in the place of a king. In New Testament times, however, the Sanhedrin served as the final court of authority for the Jews. Outside of court, an official with authority to pronounce judgment in legal cases served as "judge." Bribing such a judge was not uncommon, so the rich and powerful often received no punishment for their wrongdoing. Meanwhile, defenseless widows, orphans, and handicapped received little or no justice.[1]

The Bible places widows in a special category of concern, compassion, and consideration. The early church was warned to "give proper recognition to those widows who are really in need" (1 Tim. 5:3 f.) A widow was legally defenseless and an object of charity and public compassion. The law and the prophets commanded the people of Israel to give merciful consideration to widows (Deut. 14:29).[2] "In all codes but the Hebrew, where she is generally ignored, she has rights of inheritance."[3] The Old Testament prophets constantly warned Israel against mistreatment of widows and the underprivileged. Numerous Old and New Testament warnings seemed to suggest that inferior treatment, injustice, and lack of mercy were usually received by widows. Early Christians did organize to care for Greek widows (Acts 6:1f.), for acceptable service to God included serving the needs of widows (James 1:27).

The Persistent Widow *(Luke 18:1-8)*

Jesus wanted his followers to make room for God in their lives. He stressed the many ways God acts in the world, the many ways God can be reached, and the many ways God responds. Jesus wanted his disciples to be assured and secure in their knowledge of God, so he told this parable:

A judge who lived in a certain town did not care about people. His verdicts were unjust, and he dispensed justice to those who bribed him. Needless to say, he cared little about God. In that same town, however, there lived a widow who found herself totally defenseless because of her inferior position in the community. She was an object of charity and had absolutely no recourse in a legal settlement, except to throw herself on the mercy of the judge. One day, this widow was among those who came to the unjust judge for help. She pleaded, "Help me, judge. Please decide in my favor." The judge ignored her pleas, for he didn't care about her or anyone else. But the next time he held court, she came again and pleaded with him, "Please judge, grant me justice against my adversary." Again he ignored her, showing no concern for her problem. The next time his court convened the judge found her before him once again. "Please grant me justice against my opponent," she pleaded. But still he ignored her. Thereafter, each time the judge held court she was there in the room crying and pleading for assistance. Finally, the judge gave up. He reasoned, "the only way to keep this woman from bothering me is to give her what she wants." So he gave her justice.

And then Jesus turned and told his apostles, "If an inconsiderate, insensitive, and unjust judge can be moved by the persistent pleas of a widow, will not a loving God bring justice to his own people?" Jesus constantly stressed that we serve a King who *cares* and can be moved by the pleas of our hearts. God is touched in his very inner being by our guilt, hurts, and lostness. Because he cares, he is moved to action within our own lives. Thus, Christians serve "a King who cares."

Bread At Midnight

Travel by night is still common in the Middle East due to the intense daytime heat. I have traveled at various times of the day and night in several countries of the Middle East and found that even at night there may be few breezes. Because of this travel custom, the arrival of a friend at the home of his host in the middle of the night would not be uncommon.

Custom would call for the host to set a full meal before his arriving guests. And the meal might become a community project.

Village women cooperate in bread baking, and it is known who has baked recently. There may be some bread left in the host's house, but he must offer the guest a complete unbroken loaf. To feed a guest with a partial loaf left from another meal would be an insult.[4]

Even today, three full loaves are regarded as necessary for a meal for one person.[5]

The host could be confident in borrowing from his neighbors to help him feed his guest. This confidence was based upon the fact "that the guest is guest of the *community*, not just of the individual . . . . In going to his neighbor, the host is asking the sleeper to fulfill his duty to the guest of the village."[6] Refusal to help in the entertainment of a guest would be unimaginable to a Palestinian. Bread at midnight for a guest would be necessary under any circumstances.

The Persistent Host *(Luke 11:5-10)*

After Jesus finished praying one day, his disciples asked him to teach them to pray. Jesus gave them what has come to be called "The Lord's Prayer." Afterwards, he told them a parable that assured his disciples of their constant access to God.

Suppose a man has an unexpected visit in the middle of the night by a friend. Realizing he is the host, suppose the man goes to a neighbor at midnight and breaks the quietness of the night with a loud knock crying, "Friend, lend me some bread to help feed my guest. I don't have enough food to serve him." But suppose the neighbor answers, "Go away, don't bother me. I've already locked the door. Besides, my family is asleep, so

161

I can't get up and give you anything." Now, suppose the host doesn't give up but continues to plead with his neighbor over and over. You know what the neighbor will do, don't you! Because of the man's persistence, the neighbor will get up and give him whatever he needs.

Then Jesus turned to his disciples and explained that they could approach God because he is "our Father." We don't have to approach God as though we were inconveniencing him. Thus, Jesus said:

> Ask and it will be given to you; seek and you will find; knock and the door will be opened to you. For everyone who asks receives; he who seeks finds; and to him who knocks, the door will be opened.
>
> Luke 11:9-10

Jesus then said it another way. No human father would trick his own children by giving them evil when they asked for good. Our perfect father in heaven readily gives the Holy Spirit to those who ask him (Luke 11:11-13). Jesus taught that the God to whom we pray will never contradict his loving nature. He is truly a "King who cares."

The Power Of Prayer

One of the great mysteries of our relationship to God is how we as finite human beings can affect the infinite God of the universe. Yet, the Scripture is alive with examples of the power of prayer. Each time the lesson is that through prayer God's person can affect his great heart.

When God decided to destroy the city of Sodom, Abraham prayed to God for the salvation of just a few people. His prayer affected God (Gen. 18:24 ff.).

Again, when God saw the people of Israel worshiping a golden calf, he decided that they would be destroyed. But Moses prayed to God, and his prayer affected the great heart of God. The people of Israel remained the people of God (Exod. 32:31 ff.).

When King Hezekiah was told to prepare himself for death, he prayed to God. His prayer affected the great heart of God, who granted Hezekiah fifteen more years of leadership (2 Kings 20:3 ff.).

"The prayer of a righteous man is powerful and effective" (James 5:16b).

". . . prayer affects God . . . due to the bold confidence of God's disciples."

Why does prayer affect God? The answer seems to lie in the *nature of God*. If even hard-hearted human beings will respond to persistent pleading, begging, and requesting, then God, who cares more than any human being, can be affected by persistent prayer. It is his nature to *care*, and prayer is fundamentally built upon God's nature.

A second reason prayer affects God is due to the *bold confidence of God's disciple*. Jesus stressed in each of these parables the "persistence" of the beggar, of the one pleading. The Greek word for "persistence" is used only this once in the New

Testament, and its meaning literally is "lack of shame."[7] We should not think of persistence as nagging or as badgering, which are negative traits. It is to be understood as constancy and boldness, very positive attributes. "Let us then approach the throne of grace with confidence, so that we may receive mercy and find grace to help us in our time of need" (Heb. 4:16).

Because a disciple knows he can come boldly to God as his "Father," prayer has tremendous power.

A God Who Cares

"God's gonna getcha if you don't watch out," claims modern man. For many, God is a monstrous being who causes freeway accidents, brings diseases, and sends death upon people. But Jesus showed that God relates to people as a *father* relates to his own children.

When all of the circumstances of life seem to be going against us and the doors of life are locked, we can be certain that God cares for us. He is never too busy, far away, or inaccessable. The cries of God's people touch his heart. We can learn to depend upon him to deliver us from tribulations. In the "midnights" of our own personal lives, God will come to the door and give us what we need.

Jesus urges his disciples to "ask" of God in their prayers. We can ask of God because he is our Father and friend. The promise and guarantee of Jesus is that "everyone who asks receives." We ask because we feel a need. When we feel deep need, God is there to give us what he knows is best for us.

Jesus implores us to "seek" God. We must seek him because we believe he's there and that he has a will for our lives. We seek because we believe he has the answer to our problems. The promise of Jesus is that "he who seeks finds." There is no doubt, nor hesitation, on the part of Jesus. When out of deep need we seek the will of God, we can find it.

Finally, Jesus implores us to "knock," to take action. He wants us to never give up nor ever be ashamed or embarrassed to ask, but rather to be persistent and constant in our prayer life. Even though the door may be locked, the promise of Jesus is that it "will be opened" when we knock.

"In the 'midnights' of our own personal lives, God will come to the door and give us what we need."

In God we have a Father, a friend, and a King who cares. The injunction of Jesus is to pray persistently to God, bringing him your personal needs—for he truly cares!

Who Can We Trust?

In 1972, I had the privilege of serving as an observer at the National Political Conventions in Miami Beach. During my interviews with hundreds of Democrats, I heard them saying, "You can't trust a Republican." During similar interviews with many Republicans, I heard them saying, "You can't trust a Democrat." "Believability" or "credibility" has come to be a real problem in the world of politics. In a world of phone taps, cover-ups, broken promises, contracts with small print, and laws with exceptions, it is difficult for a person to believe or to trust.

Is there someone who always tells the truth? Is there someone whose nature can be counted upon as being solid and firm? Is there anyone whose promise is so certain, so secure, that you can always believe it? Is there someone who doesn't seem to have a "credibility problem"? Is there someone who doesn't forget, fail, or cover-up? The major reason that we can be persistent in our prayers is that God *promises* to answer our prayer. Whenever we "ask," "seek," or "knock," we are given the promise of God that we will receive, find, and enter into blessings (Luke 11:9-10). What backs up God's promise to answer our prayers? Scripture claims that God's promises are backed up by his "faithfulness." God is described as "the faithful God" (Deut. 7:9). "Great is your faithfulness" (Lam. 3:23) is said of God. Twice in 1 Corinthians Paul claims that "God is faithful" (1 Cor. 1:9; 10:13). "He who promised is faithful" (Heb. 10:23b). "Faithfulness" is our grounds for assurance and confidence in believing that God will answer our prayers.

A Name You Can Trust

How does God demonstrate his faithfulness in answering our prayers? God demonstrates his "credibility" to man by his reputation, good name, and character. Through his experiences with people, God shows that he has a faithful reputation. God promised Abraham a son, land,

and a great nation; and he kept his promise (Gen. 12:1-3; 22:15-18). He renewed his promises of presents, blessings, and territory to Isaac and kept his promises (Gen. 26:1-5). David had the promise of God's covenant (2 Sam. 7:4-17; Ps. 89:3, 4, 35-37). God promised King Solomon that He would give him special guidance, and He did (1 Kings 3:5-14; 2 Chron. 1:7-12). In short, by keeping his personal promises to different people, God shows that he can be depended upon.

"Behind each of God's promises is his unchanging and constant nature."

God also demonstrates his faithfulness through the power of his good name. The name of God was held in deep reverence and was not usually pronounced by the ancient Hebrews. Variations upon the name "Jehovah" show the outstanding attributes of God's good name. The name "Jehovah-Jireh" means "the Lord will provide" (Gen. 22:14). "Jehovah-Rophi" means that God is "the miracle leader" (Exod. 15:26). "Jehovah-Shalom" means "the Lord is our peace" (Judg. 6:24). "Jehovah-Rohi" means "the Lord is my Redeemer" (Isa. 44:24). These are just a few of the many instances in the scripture where the very name of God shows his faithfulness, reliability, and trustworthiness.

The faithfulness of God is also demonstrated by his character. Behind each of God's promises is his unchanging and constant nature.

Because God wanted to make the unchanging

nature of his purpose very clear to the heirs of what was promised, he confirmed it with an oath. God did this so that, by two unchangeable things in which it is impossible for God to lie, we who have fled to take hold of the hope offered to us may be greatly encouraged.

Hebrews 6:17-18

And Peter claims that "the Lord is not slow in keeping his promise . . . " (2 Peter 3:9). God will always answer a prayer in perfect harmony with his nature. He is love, truth, power, and a King who cares.

Jesus' great promise that God will answer our prayers calls for great faith on our part. It is said that Martin Luther once was overwhelmed by the faithfulness of God and wrote, "I forgot God when I said, 'How can this be?' " Let us not forget God today—he's our Father.

---

[1] For additional background reading on the role of a judge, see G.T. Manley, "Judges," *The New Bible Dictionary* (Grand Rapids: William B. Eerdmans Publishing Co., 1975), p. 676; C.U. Wolf, "Judge," *The Interpreter's Dictionary of the Bible*, Vol. 2 (Nashville: Abingdon Press, 1962), pp. 1012-1013.

[2] Steven Barabus, "Widow," *The Zondervan Pictorial Bible Dictionary* (Grand Rapids: Zondervan Publishing House, 1963), p. 894; O.J. Baab, "Widow," *The Interpreter's Dictionary of the Bible*, Vol. 4, p. 842.

[3] Loc. cit.

[4] Kenneth E. Bailey, *Poet and Peasant* (Grand Rapids: William B. Eerdmans Publishing Co., 1976), p. 122.

[5] Joachim Jeremias, *Rediscovering the Parables* (New York: Charles Scribner's Sons, 1966), p. 124.

[6] Bailey, op. cit., pp. 122-123.

[7] William F. Arndt and F. Wilbur Gingrich, "άvaideia, as, n' " *A Greek-English Lexicon of the New Testament and Other Early Christian Literature* (Chicago: The University of Chicago Press, 1957), p. 54.

Principles Of Kingdom – Life 12

A number of years ago, the head of DuPont's research division called together all of those who had worked at making and producing film. "Forget what you know about film," he told his audience of distinguished research scientists, "and see a vision of what can be done with film." Given such a challenge, these DuPont scientists began working on a new film—the strongest film ever developed. For they developed a film strong enough to pull a car.

In a similar sense, it would be helpful if we might for a moment forget what we know about the church and see a vision of what the church can be. I love the church. Its vitality, excitement, and enthusiasm give the Christian life its sense of adventure. Yet the deadness, darkness, and despair of some congregations contrast greatly with the life and light of the New Testament church. We need to dream a dream of what the church really can be.

In his parables, Jesus has given us a beautiful glimpse of genuine Christianity, not counterfeit

169

Christianity. He has taught us the principles of kingdom life—the mysteries of the kingdom of heaven. "He who has ears, let him hear," Jesus warned (Matt. 13:9).

Today we live in a tension between his first and second coming. Jesus still invites us to look through spiritual eyes to the principles and strategies of God, which are at work between his birth and his final coming. In two of his parables, Jesus dealt with the way we live between the times. In his revealing of the secrets of kingdom—life, we are allowed to see "the things hidden since the creation of the world" (Matt. 13:35).

Before turning to each of these parables on kingdom—life, it is helpful to understand that the meaning of these parables was not always clear to those who heard them. Jesus explained that "the knowledge of the secrets of the kingdom of heaven has been given to you, but not to them" (Matt. 13:11). Then, he unveiled for us the operational principle by which God allows men to understand the principles of kingdom—life: Whoever acts on the truth he has will receive more; whoever does not act will lose the truth he has (Matt. 13:12).

Weeds

"Tares" were an annual bearded darnel, a poisonous rye grass that was very common in the Middle East. Commonly found in wheat fields, it looked almost exactly like wheat until the ear appeared. The roots of tares would creep underground and become intertwined with those of the wheat. Consequently, if the darnel was pulled up, so was the wheat. Because tares were noxious, the wheat had to be separated from it at harvest. After harvest, the wheat was fanned and then put through a sieve. The smaller darnel seeds left after fanning passed through the sieve, leaving the wheat behind.[1] In some instances, women and children were given the tedious, manual task of separating the wheat from the darnel.[2] The tares were bound into bundles and burned—not as waste but as fuel.[3]

The Weeds And The Wheat
(Matt. 13:24-30; 36-43)

One day as Jesus sat by the Sea of Galilee, large crowds gathered to hear him speak about kingdom—life. Even though he knew not everyone of the hearers would understand, he knew, nevertheless, that some in his audience would see and respond.

A man plowed his soil and prepared his field for sowing. He then sowed good wheat seed in his prepared field. But one night the man's enemy came and sowed darnel among the wheat. Of course, there was no way to tell that the wheat and the darnel were not the same until the blades appeared.

The owner's servants came to him and said, "Where did the darnel come from? Didn't we sow good wheat seed in the field?" The owner replied, "My enemy did this, perhaps, out of revenge."

The servants then asked the owner of the wheat field, "Do you want us to go and pull up the darnel?" "No," he answered, "because damage will result to the wheat by premature separation. Let them both grow together until the harvest. And at that time I'll tell the harvesters to first collect the darnel and tie them in bundles to be burned and then to gather the wheat and bring it into my barns."

When Jesus finished the parable, the crowd left. Then his disciples said to him, "Explain to us the parable of the weeds in the field." And he answered:

The one who sowed the good seed is the Son of Man. The field is the world, and the good seed stands for the sons of the kingdom. The weeds are the sons of the evil one, and the enemy who sows them is the devil. The harvest is the end of the age, and the harvesters are angels. As the weeds are pulled up and burned in the fire, so it will be at the end of the age. The Son of Man will send out his angels, and they will weed out of his kingdom everything that causes sin and all who do evil. They will throw them into the fiery furnace, where there will be weeping and grinding of teeth. Then the righteous will shine like the sun in the kingdom of their Father. He who has ears, let him hear.

Matthew 13:37-43

Seine-Nets And Fishes

One of the most lucrative industries in ancient Israel was fishing, which provided a favorite food for the Jews. Even today, the fish from the Sea of Galilee is a delicacy on tables throughout the Middle East. So important was the fishing industry that one of the gates in Jerusalem was called "the fish-gate."[4]

172

The New Testament describes several scenes of fishermen washing, mending, or casting their nets. The seine net is a special kind of dragnet by which several fishermen cover a bed of fish with the net and then drag it to shore. The seine net "is either dragged between two boats or laid out by a single boat and pulled to the land with long ropes."[5] When the seine net was pulled to shore, the fishermen began to separate the "clean" fish from the "unclean" fish. According to Leviticus 11:9-12 and Deuteronomy 14:9-10, "clean" fish were those having scales and fins, while "unclean" fish were those without fins and scales, such as shell fish.[6]

The Seine-Net *(Matt. 13:47-52)*

In order to unveil the secrets of kingdom—life, Jesus told the parable of the seine net.

One day a large number of fishermen took their dragnet and let it down into the lake. They began to drag it through the waters of the lake toward the shoreline. When the dragnet was full, the fishermen pulled it upon the shore. Then, they sat down and began to collect the clean fish into baskets. But they threw the unclean fish away.

Jesus then turned to his disciples and told them, "This is how it will be at the end of the age. The angels will come and separate the wicked from the righteous and throw them into the fiery furnace, where there will be weeping and gnashing of teeth" (Matt. 13:49-50).

Organic Growth

A basic principle of kingdom—life is the following: the kingdom of God grows slowly and gradually, like all other living things, and by *organic development*. In the parable of the weeds, Jesus tells us that " . . . the good seed stands for the sons of the kingdom" (Matt. 13:38). As we open our hearts to God's rule, we are planted in the world. It is a mystery of kingdom—life that although no fruit is yet apparent, God's rule has been sown among the people of the earth. God then works by his own time frame. He calls on his workers to have patience and perserverance so growth may take place.

"Growth takes place when a faithful life reproduces itself."

. How does growth take place in the kingdom? Since the time of Jesus, many have expected the kingdom to come with dramatic catastrophe, not by gradual growth. They have predicted the second coming of Jesus over and over. Those who have held this view have missed a fundamental truth of kingdom—life. For the kingdom of God grows like other living things—by organic development. Growth takes place when a faithful life reproduces itself. In fact, the biological test for growth is whether or not an organism can reproduce itself. Church growth takes place when faithful workers in the kingdom reproduce the rule of God in other receptive, open lives.

Growth is from seed time to harvest time. So when God's rule takes root and changes the whole life of another person, God then takes that life and plants it in the world. The life of the seed is powerful. The influence, character, and actions of a faithful disciple work into the receptive lives of others. Certainly, the growth is slow! It is gradual! It is like all other living things—by organic development.

Leave The Gardening To God

Another principle of kingdom—life surfaced in the parable of the weeds: *attempts to purify the kingdom must be left to God, the Gardener.* In the parable of the weeds, the servant asked the master, "Do you want us to go and pull the weeds up?" "No," the master answered, "because while you are pulling the weeds, you may root up the wheat with them. Let both grow together until the harvest . . . " (Matt. 13:28-30). Without question, the work of Satan intrudes into the work of the kingdom. Among the many hindrances to the growth of the kingdom are:

* The dead weight of secularism.
* Apathy
* Division
* Malicious evil
* A fault-finding spirit
* A spiritual inferiority complex

"God is the gardener, not man nor any group of men."

No doubt, Satan has planted his own people in the kingdom. This basic principle of kingdom—life is one that Christian people have failed to see.

Human efforts to purify the church always fail! From the Donatists (4th century A.D.), who tried to purify the church of heresy, to the modern zealots, damage is always done to the church. God never commends irresponsible zeal! Neither does God commend impatience! God never commends those who try to take over his place. He has no compliments for those who try to appear holier than he is. God is the gardener, not man nor any group of men. If we will allow God to be God, he will purify his own kingdom in his own time and in his own way: "The Son of Man will send out his angels, and they will weed out of his kingdom everything that causes sin and all who do evil" (Matt. 13:41).

Faithful In Heart

The parables of the weeds and the seine net point us to another fundamental principle of kingdom—life: *it is the task of the people of God to be faithful in heart.* When the Bible uses the word "heart," it does not refer to the physical muscle that pumps blood to the body. Instead, the "heart of man" is the very center of man's inner life and the source of his will power. "The heart," writes Kittel, "is supremely the one centre in man to which God turns, in which the religious life is rooted, which determines moral conduct."[7] The heart is the place in man where God's Spirit convinces man's spirit that God should rule man: "For it is with your heart that you believe and are justified . . . " (Rom. 10:10). Jesus says that the message about the kingdom is "sown in a person's heart" (Matt. 13:19).

The difference between the wheat and the darnel or the clean fish and the unclean fish is a difference in heart condition. For when God's rule takes root in a receptive, contrite, open, and broken heart the process of salvation begins. It reaches its climax in harvest time. For Jesus, the issue is never in doubt! Harvest time is inherent in the seed. Christ breaks through and into a person's life by coming into his heart. The task of that person's life is to be faithful in heart.

What is the future of the kingdom of God? Think for a few minutes of what the church can be. Do everything within your own power to see that the kingdom is a victorious reality in the lives of people.

---

[1] John L. Leedy, "Plants of the Bible: Tares," *The Zondervan Pictorial Bible Dictionary* (Grand Rapids: Zondervan Publishing House, 1963), p. 668.

[2] J.D. Douglas, ed., "Tares," *The New Bible Dictionary* (Grand Rapids: William B. Eerdmans Publishing Co., 1975), p. 1238.

[3] Joachim Jeremias, *Rediscovering The Parables* (New York: Charles Scribner's Sons, 1966), p. 177.

[4] Alfred Edersheim, *The Life and Times of Jesus The Messiah*, Vol. 1 (Grand Rapids: William B. Eerdmans Publishing Co., 1953), p. 473.

[5] Jeremias, op. cit., p. 177.

[6] J.A. Thompson, "Fish, Fishing," *The New Bible Dictionary*, p. 424.

[7] Behm, "Kapdia" *Theological Dictionary of the New Testament*, Vol. 3 (Grand Rapids: William B. Eerdmans Publishing Co., 1965), p. 612.

You Can't Go Around Jerusalem 13

Bookstores today are filled with paperbacks whose titles begin *"Ten Easy Steps To..."* Often the authors of these books describe their own magic, pushbutton approach to very difficult problems. Usually they promise quick success if the reader will only master their *Ten Easy Steps*. It doesn't seem to matter what the problem is—anything from making million dollars to becoming an effective public speaker. Many people are fair game for the promise of *Ten Easy Steps*. It's not particularly surprising that so many readers seem to believe that mastery of any particular task can be attained without painstaking effort.

One of the most alluring temptations we ever face is the desire to overcome a mountainous challenge by going around rather than climbing over it. It is the temptation to search for easy answers to hard problems, to believe that a magic pushbutton exists for every demanding undertaking. It is the temptation to stare truth in the face and to be tempted to back away from it, rather than to submit to it. It is to believe that the successful people in life are those who have been lifted to the clouds on flowery beds of ease. It is to think that every complexity has a shortcut method.

This temptation pulls at all of us all too readily, as we can see in the constant mass advertising that competes for our values, our attention, and our money. Ads from cars to colognes promise, "Buy me, use me, own me; and I will make you an instant success. Without any effort on your part, I will make you completely happy. You deserve the very best."

So many of us want easy answers to the most difficult questions of life: "Who am I? Where did I come from? How am I to live? Where am I going?" If some of us were to read a sign saying, "The escalator to success is out of order; please climb the stairs," we'd sit down instead and wait for the repairman.

No wonder this state of mind finds a stumbling block to what Jesus taught. The central symbol for discipleship in the kingdom is not an escalator but a cross! And what that cross means is clear and unmistakable to us: life comes through death; victory comes through loss. Jesus taught us to discuss our own potentialities of life, love, and service in the kingdom, not by asking us to sit on cozy pews of ease but by demanding us to sacrifice ourselves on a cross of self-denial. Jesus teaches that this paradox of the cross is a Jerusalem that we can't escape.

The Symbol of "Jerusalem"

Luke used the city of Jerusalem as a symbol of this paradox in his gospel. As he painted his portrait of Jesus in Galilee, his strokes revealed an idyllic, peaceful, restful, and even pastoral ministry. In the opening part, he portrayed Jesus as very popular. His ministry avoided confrontation and struggle (Luke 1:1–9:50). But at Luke 9:51, the writer provided a pivot, a turning point, in his portrait of Jesus: "As the time approached for him to be taken up to heaven, Jesus resolutely set out for Jerusalem." From this point on, Luke began reminding us of Jerusalem and Jesus' journey to the climactic events in Jerusalem.

"Jesus gave Jerusalem a new symbolic meaning of suffering, service, death, and resurrection."

Luke referred so often, so deliberately, to Jerusalem that it came to mean something more than simply a city in Judea. It came to symbolize a particular experience that Jesus would have. For instance, the Samaritans would not accept Jesus because he was "heading for Jerusalem" (Luke 9:53). Later, Jesus had to teach his apostles that they didn't have time to wipe out a Samaritan village—because they were going to Jerusalem. In Luke's narrative, only those "going to Jerusalem" would know such urgency: ". . . Jesus went through the towns and villages, teaching as he made his way to Jerusalem" (Luke 13:22). For

Jesus, time was at a premium, the opportunity became limited, and people must be taught about God as he moved toward Jerusalem. Again, Luke showed Jesus serving the needs of people and of healing lepers as he traveled between Samaria and Galilee "on his way to Jerusalem" (Luke 17:11). Jesus served the cripple, the blind, and the children as he made his way toward Jerusalem. Jesus gave Jerusalem a new, symbolic meaning of suffering, service, death, and resurrection. He addressed his apostles:

> We are going up to Jerusalem, and everything that is written by the prophets about the son of man will be fulfilled. He will be handed over to the Gentiles. They will mock him, insult him, spit on him, flog him, and kill him. On the third day he will rise again.
>
> Luke 18:31-33

For more than three years, Jesus had moved in the provinces around Jerusalem. But Jerusalem itself had not really been challenged since the days of the prophets. Jesus had neither penetrated nor experienced Jerusalem. At the right moment, he decided that if he was to become the Savior and Lord of all who would accept him, he had to go to Jerusalem. In order to accomplish his divine mission, there came a time when Jesus could no longer stay in the outlying provinces.

The "Jerusalem" Parables

Sometimes the parables of Jesus appear in no particular sequence in the Gospels—almost standing on their own with no particular reference to the context in which they are found.

Other times the location of a parable seems especially significant. This is true of what we shall call the "Jerusalem" parables, the parable of the ten minas and the parable of the talents.

"The 'Jerusalem' parables deal with the bedrock issue—the question of Jesus' authority."

Luke included them in his narrative of Jesus going to Jerusalem. In his introduction to the parable of the ten minas, Luke wrote that Jesus " . . . went on to tell them a parable, because he was near Jerusalem and the people thought that the kingdom of God was going to appear at once" (Luke 19:11). Luke then wrote that when Jesus finished the parable of the ten minas, " . . . he went on ahead, going up to Jerusalem" (Luke 19:28). Furthermore, Jesus told the parable of the tenants in the Jerusalem temple just after he had cleaned the temple. Luke viewed the event as part of Jesus' major confrontation with the chief priests, teachers of the law, and Jewish elders. So for Luke, the Jerusalem motif established the setting for both parable. They have the distinction of being the last parables that Jesus told. Only Luke recorded them both—though Matthew (21:33-46) and Mark (12:1-12) did record the parable of the tenants.

The "Jerusalem" parables deal with the bedrock issue—the question of Jesus' authority. The quiet, peaceful, and pastoral days of Galilee had passed. We sense the confrontation, directness, and chal-

lenge of the Jewish religious leaders in their ultimate question, " . . . Who gave you this authority?" (Luke 20:2). That question is the essential
one for understanding Jesus and his kingdom.
They in effect asked, "How dare you make such
claims and perform such deeds? How do you
justify what you say and do? Since all authority is
either from God or from men, which do you claim
to be?" Their questions came right between the
two Jerusalem parables. In Jerusalem, Jesus
clearly declared through these two parables who
he was and the source of his authority.

Minas And Tenants

At the time of Jesus, Greek money circulated
along with Jewish coins. The basic Greek silver
coin was the *drachma*. One hundred *drachmas*
equaled one *mina*, which was worth about sixteen
dollars. So 100 *minae* would be about sixteen hundred dollars—several years wages in New Testament times. (A *mina* was considered to be about
three months wages. Whereas some of the Greek
coins increased in value with the changes in economy, the *mina* lost value. The *drachma*, the basis
for the value of the *mina*, depreciated about sixteen cents under the early Caesars.[1])

Those who have studied ancient economics tell
us that Jewish law differentiated between commerical interest and increase. In fact, the Old
Testament prohibited commercial interest (Exod.
22:25). But by New Testament times, the economy
had changed and fair business practices allowed
return on commerical investments. Customarily,
bankers placed money out at interest rates between four and eight percent.[2]

The Ten Minas *(Luke 19:11-27)* **And The Tenants**
(Luke 20:9-19)

As Jesus approached Jerusalem, he spoke with
directness, even sharpness. The crowds he drew
included not only the loyal followers but the
curious, the doubters, the impatient, and the
stubborn as well. Among those listening to him
were some who rejected his authority and who
refused to submit to his lordship. To all who
heard him during these times, he stressed the
need for faithful service in his kingdom, as well as
his own authority as king. Both themes appear in
this story:

**A man with abilities to rule decided he would
go to a country and live among the citizens of
that country to become their king. After being
invested with the right to rule, he planned to
return. Before he left, he called ten of his servants and entrusted each with three months
wages—a considerable amount of money. He in-
structed each to make a capital investment so that
when he returned the principal would have
gained interest or even more.**

**Meanwhile, some of his fellow citizens re-
fused to accept his right to rule over their lives;
and they objected by saying, "We don't want this
man to be our king." He, however, became their
king with all the rights and privileges of his
position.**

**Upon returning home, he called in all of his
servants so that they might give an account of
their investment. The first servant had wisely
considered his financial opportunities, had in-**

vested, and returned to his king 100 percent on his original investment. The king rewarded his faithful servant by placing him in charge of ten cities in his kingdom. Likewise, the second servant had invested wisely and returned 50 percent on his original investment. The king placed him over five cities for his faithful service. The third servant, however, failed to use his opportunity, his master's original investment, and returned it to him without any increase. The king rebuked him for not using his opportunity and gave the unfaithful servant's original amount to the servant who had been the most diligent.

The king then sent for those who had rebelled at his kingship and had defied his right to rule. He executed extreme judgment toward them.

In this parable, Jesus insisted on faithful service in the kingdom; but beyond that, he predicted the downfall of those who would refuse his credentials and defy his kingship. To those who decided they were the ultimate authority for their own lives and had no need for Jesus as Lord, he undercut both their rights and their power to do so. He, therefore, exposed their intrigue and opposition to his lordship. This parable proved to be a dangerous one, for it stirred up the anger of his opposition.

The first two servants in the story represent those who accept the authority of Jesus for their lives and render faithful service in his kingdom. The third servant, however, typifies the person who claims to be religious, yet hoards the treasures of God. In the original setting, this servant corresponded to the Jewish leaders, who had been entrusted with a considerable spiritual fortune—the rite of circumcision, the law of Moses, a history of redemption, a chosen people. But they had to accept the right of Christ to rule over their lives. Thus, they brought the Lord no increase on the original investment he had given them. The parable warns that a time of accounting is coming when the king of glory will execute judgment. "All authority in heaven and on earth," he said, "has been given to me" (Matt. 28:18).

After telling this parable, Jesus went on to Jerusalem. There he cleared the temple of religious profiteers and taught daily in the temple. Yet, the Jewish leaders challenged his authority to do any of this. Their challenge issued in a clash of human authority with God's authority, of man's attempt to usurp God's power. The clash provided Jesus with a final opportunity to tell them a story, a parable of confrontation.

A man planted a vineyard and rented it to some tenants with whom he made an arrangement. At harvest time, they were to take part of the grapes as payment and pay him a share of the harvest. He then went away for a long time on a journey. When the produce from the vineyard began to come in, he sent one of his servants to the tenants to collect his share of the harvest. But the unprincipled tenants decided to take advantage of the owner, who lived at a distance. So they beat the servant and sent him away with none of the harvest.

The owner sent another servant, whom the tenants beat and treated shamefully. The owner

then sent a third servant, and they paid him with injuries and threw him out.

The owner decided that such severe actions on the part of his tenants deserved the most extreme response. He decided to solve the problem by sending his beloved son to the tenants. He thought they would respect him. But the rebellion of the tenants was so great that they decided to kill the son so the vineyard might be theirs. So the son suffered and died.

"What then will the owner of the vineyard do to them?" asks Jesus. He will execute judgment on those tenants and give the vineyard to other people.

Here Jesus drew a symbolic picture of Israel's long, religious history. This parable may have reminded the Jews of Isaiah's picture of Israel as the vineyard of God (Isa. 5:1-7). God repeatedly extends his long-suffering toward them by sending his prophets, his messengers, and even John the Baptist. But Jerusalem continued to refuse his messengers. The climax of the relationship between Israel and God neared as the heir, God's son, was soon to be killed in Jerusalem. No wonder when Jesus approaches Jerusalem and sees the city, he weeps over it. (Luke 19:41).

When Jesus was crucified in Jerusalem, the limitations of man's power was revealed. But man's power is always momentary, while God's power is permanent. Jesus was buried in a tomb, but he did not remain in that tomb. He became the only person in history to live, to die, to live again, and to never die! He demonstrated his final authority in all things. To do so, he had to go through Jerusalem, not around it.

"Jerusalem" Means A Cross

The cross is at the center of understanding Jesus and the nature of his kingdom. Throughout his ministry, Jesus spoke of being a king and of having a kingdom. But he did not have in mind an earthly nation with political power strong enough to rule Rome and the whole earth. His followers, especially his apostles, had a great deal of difficulty in understanding this. They continued to misunderstand him and were not sure about him. At his transfiguration, they suggested building a shelter. Not sure of his power, they didn't know where they would get enough food to feed the multitudes. They overlooked the presence of the Creator of everything who was standing right beside them.

The nature of his kingdom was an even greater mystery to them. They struggled for seats of power in his coming kingdom, and they wanted to rule over each other. But Jesus wanted them to know that his kingdom is God's acceptance of the unacceptable. It is the rule of God in the hearts and lives of rejected people, who are conscious of their guilt and need of forgiveness and who willingly obey God. To the disciples who argued over greatness, he showed that the way to the kingdom is through humbling oneself. Even though they kept missing the point about life in the kingdom, Jesus never gave up on them.

Largely rejected by the religious leaders, who supposedly were able to understand the history and work of God among the Jews, Jesus turned to the despised, the simple, and the guilt-ridden. He offered them forgiveness and the possibility of becoming a joint-heir in his kingdom.

"The kingdom of God is God's effort to restore a lost relationship between man and God."

But in order for the kingdom of God to take place in human lives, Jesus had to suffer and die on the cross. His behaviour while going to Jerusalem, even his suffering and dying, has the character of a sign. For Jesus, going through Jerusalem meant:

* Total commitment to do God's will rather than his own.
* Serving the real needs of real people.
* Confronting religious merchants and disassociating himself from them.
* Suffering and dying on a cross.
* Rising from the tomb on the third day.

So the kingdom of God is God's effort to restore a lost relationship between man and God. To attain this end, Jesus had to go to Jerusalem. That meant he was to suffer, give hope, confront, struggle, serve, and die. When we realize that Jesus went to such length to give us a new way of living, we begin to realize the nature of his kingship and kingdom and our call.

We Are Called To "Jerusalem"

Jesus calls us today to follow him. And when

190

we do, the journey ultimately leads us, too, to Jerusalem. For there is a Jerusalem in every Christian journey. He is always ahead of us, calling for us to follow.

> And so Jesus also suffered outside the city gate to make his people holy through his own blood. Let us, then go to him outside the camp, bearing the disgrace he bore. For here we do not have an enduring city, but we are looking for the city that is to come.
>
> Hebrews 13:12-14

"By going to Jerusalem and dying, we find life."

Jesus calls us to follow him to Jerusalem. When we follow him there, we set aside out own inwardness and go out to be with people. That's where Jesus is. He wants us to be among his children, friends, the depressed, men, women, the suffering, and the hurting. He wants us to offer the rule of God to such people and to call upon them to respond to him. He wants us to disassociate ourselves from the religious profiteers, who keep people form seeing the beauty and power of God and his church. He calls us to carry a cross and offers it to us. In the end, the people of God can't go around Jerusalem!

By going to Jerusalem and dying, we find life. By surrendering to a cross in Jerusalem, we become victors and conquerors. By giving up our lives on crosses of service, we find the ultimate joy of our faith. It's the paradox of the kingdom of

God. It mystified the apostles; the religious leaders stumbled at it. Today, the call of Jerusalem is still the same. Our choice is still the same: go around it and live a life of evasion; or go through it and discover a life of victory.

---

[1] J.D. Douglas, ed., *The New Bible Dictionary* (Grand Rapids: William B. Eerdman's Publishing Company, 1975), p. 840; John D. Davis, *The Westminister Dictionary of The Bible* (Philadelphia: The Westminster Press, 1944), p. 405.

[2] Alfred Edersheim, *The Life and Times of Jesus The Messiah*, Vol. 2 (Grand Rapids: William B. Eerdman's Publishing Company, 1953), pp. 463-464.